OUTRAGEOUS
WOMEN
OF THE
AMERICAN FRONTIER

Mary Rodd Furbee

John Wiley & Sons, Inc.

Special thanks to three wise and talented people:
Jane Yolen, Betts Rodd, Tom Rodd.

This book is printed on acid-free paper. ∞

Copyright © 2002 by Mary Rodd Furbee. All rights reserved

Maps on pages viii, 32, and 68 copyright © 2002 by Jessica Wolk-Stanley

Published by John Wiley & Sons, Inc., New York
Published simultaneously in Canada

Design and production by Navta Associates, Inc.

This publication is designed to provide accurate and authoritative information in regard to the subject matter covered. It is sold with the understanding that the publisher is not engaged in rendering legal, accounting, or other professional services. If legal advice or other expert assistance is required, the services of a competent professional person should be sought.

Library of Congress Cataloging-in-Publication Data:

Furbee, Mary R. (Mary Rodd)
   Outrageous women of the American frontier / Mary Rodd Furbee.
      p. cm.
   Includes bibliographical references (p.).
   Contents: Sacagawea—Gertrudis Barcelo—Narcissa Whitman—Juana Briones—Luzena Stanley Wilson—Eliza Roxcy Snow—Bridget "Biddy" Mason—Charlie Parkhurst—"Stagecoach" Mary Fields—Martha "Calamity Jane" Cannary—Sarah Winnemucca Hopkins—Libby Custer—Nellie Cashman—Evelyn Cameron.
   Summary: Biographies of some outspoken and influential women who lived in the American West from the late eighteenth through the early twentieth century.
   ISBN 0-471-38300-7 (acid-free paper)
     1. Women pioneers—West (U.S.)—Biography—Juvenile literature. 2. Frontier and pioneer life—West (U.S.)—Juvenile literature. 3. West (U.S.)—Biography—Juvenile literature. [1. Pioneers. 2. Women—Biography. 3. Frontier and pioneer life—West (U.S.) 4. West (U.S.)—Biography.] I. Title.

F596 .F94 2002   2001045455

Printed in the United States of America

10 9 8 7 6 5 4 3 2 1

C O N T E N T S

PART THREE. THE AGE OF EXPANSION (1870S–1900)

When you hear the words *American frontier,* what images pop into your mind? Davy Crockett and Daniel Boone forging trails through the wilderness? Sitting Bull riding on horseback by a cluster of tepees on the plain? When I was a girl, that's the frontier I learned about from history books. Women were rarely featured in those books, except for a handful of nameless motherly women peering out of covered wagons, or haggard pioneers standing in sod hovels surrounded by several grim-looking children.

From novels, movies, and television, I gained different images of frontier women. They were strong, enduring pioneers in cozy log cabins and headstrong, free-spirited girls racing across the prairie. They were feisty women doctors on horseback and sassy dance-hall girls with hearts of gold. These more modern stereotypes of frontier women made me positively nostalgic for the good old days!

Later in life, though, I discovered much about the real history of frontier women, which led me to write this book. My discoveries about the gritty realities of frontier life—bedbugs and mosquitoes, starvation and shoot-outs, ruthless treatment of Native Americans—also nipped my nostalgia in the bud. I no longer wish I had lived on the frontier, but I admire frontier women more than ever.

In nineteenth-century America there wasn't much tolerance for adventurous women with big dreams. Victorian notions that dominated "civilized" society held that women were dependent, weak, and not terribly bright. In fact, the only strength women were supposed to have was an innate goodness, which made them fit to be mothers (and, if unmarried, teachers and nurses).

(Buffalo Bill Historical Center, Cody, WY)

THE PAINTING
MADONNA OF
THE PRAIRIE
DEPICTS AN
ANGELIC FRONIER
HEROINE

Did that goodness translate into equal status in society, though? No way. Husbands, fathers, and brothers were basically the lords and masters, property owners and purse-keepers who dished out spending allowances for their womenfolk.

Still, the vast, ever-changing nineteenth-century frontier provided opportunities for women with dreams. Although not all frontier women thrived in a rugged environment, the outrageous women in this book certainly did. Each had a dream and each had true grit.

Sacagawea's dream was to find her lost family, and she enjoyed some fine adventures along the way. Missionary Narcissa Whitman's dream was to be the first white woman to travel the entire Oregon Trail. Biddy Mason's dream was to free herself from slavery and prosper as a businesswoman. Calamity Jane's dream was to break every Victorian rule about a woman's place.

The frontier era encompassed the years from 1800 to 1900. During this period, empires and immigrants vied for control of the sparsely populated landscape west of the Mississippi River. Parts of the rugged landscape of mountain ranges, deserts, and prairies were claimed by America, Britain, Spain, France, Russia, and many Native American nations.

In 1803, France sold a large section of land west of the Mississippi to America in the Louisiana Purchase. Between 1803 and the 1880s, by hook or by crook, America wrested land claims from Spain, Russia, Canada, and Native American tribes. By the late 1890s, the last Native American nations had signed treaties, had given up their land, and had agreed to settle on reservations.

By century's end, America firmly held the reins of power, from the Pacific Ocean to the Mississippi. Thousands of restless settlers and fortune seekers (the vast majority were Anglo-Saxon—Caucasian people of English, Irish, Scottish, German, and Scandinavian origin) poured into the frontier. Because whites were in the majority, American frontier history has long focused on their lives. Most white frontier immigrants were male, but the women among them left something unique: scads of diaries and letters that depicted their lives in detail.

Minority frontier women nurtured big dreams, too. African American, Native American, Hispanic, French, Russian, and Asian women sought land, fortune, freedom, and justice. For them, however, discrimination created even greater obstacles. Unfortunately, chronicling the lives of minority women is far more difficult because records are sketchy or nonexistent.

Have you ever seen a crazy quilt made from scraps of leftover fabric, each piece a unique shape, color, and texture, yet bound together into a whole? That's how I see the frontier women in this book. Some were splashy and sassy. Others were righteous and determined. Some shook their fists in anger. Others danced and sang their way through life. Stand them side by side, though, and you get a fascinating portrait of the boldest, brightest, bravest women of the American frontier.

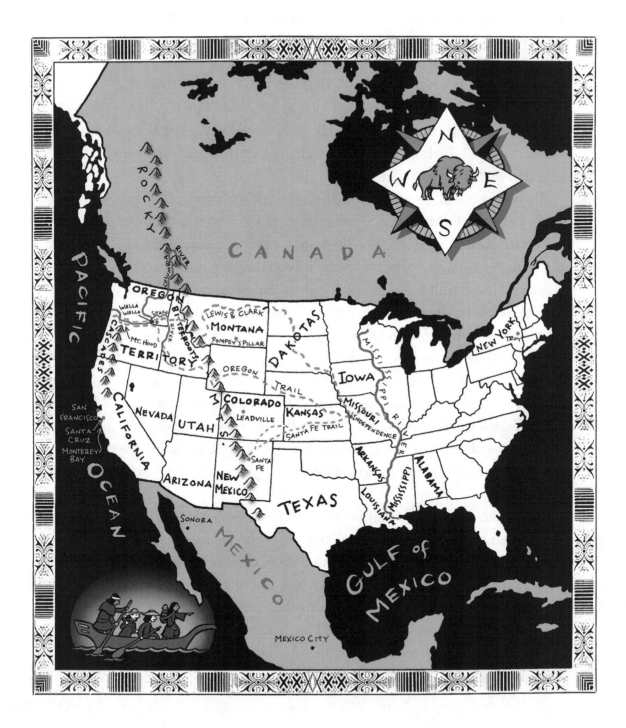

Part One

THE AGE OF CONQUEST

(1800–1840s)

AT THE DAWN *of the nineteenth century, the Mississippi River Valley marked the western boundary of the United States of America. Only a handful of explorers, traders, and missionaries had ventured deep into that mysterious wilderness. Thousands of Native American tribes dominated its vast frontier. The French also claimed a large midsection called Louisiana, the British claimed much of the Great Lakes region, the Spanish controlled most of the Southwest, and the Russians claimed parts of the Pacific Northwest. For the first few decades, this multicultural mix got along fairly well. In some areas, intermarriage was commonplace.*

In 1803, America bought the huge Louisiana territory from France for $15 million, which doubled the size of the United States. Later, this territory would become Louisiana, Arkansas, Missouri, Nebraska, South Dakota, North Dakota, Iowa, and parts of Montana, Colorado, Wyoming, Oklahoma, Mississippi, Alabama, Kansas, and Minnesota. ("Let the Land rejoice, for you have bought Louisiana for a Song," General Horatio Gates said to President Jefferson.) Then in the War of 1812, America wrested much of the Great Lakes area from Britain, and in the Pacific Northwest, America and Britain negotiated the border that separated the new Oregon Territory from Canadian lands. These victories spurred the first waves of Anglo-American settlement in the Far West and Southwest.

Meanwhile, to the south, America fought numerous battles with Mexico for control of New Mexico, Texas, Arizona, and California. Hostilities ended with the bloody Mexican-American War, which decided who would control the land. In 1848, the outnumbered, outgunned Mexican government signed the Treaty of Guadeloupe-Hidalgo, which ceded Texas, California, Arizona, New Mexico, southern portions of Nevada, Utah, and Colorado to the United States.

More than ever, Americans were convinced they were destined to control the land from sea to shining sea.

Sacagawea

(1 7 8 7 - 1 8 ? ?)

I n 1804, the famous explorers Meriwether Lewis and William Clark couldn't have opened up the 1.5-billion-acre American Northwest without a 15-year-old Shoshone girl named Sacagawea (also spelled Sacajawea). She convinced Northwest tribes that the explorers were on a mission of peace and kept the group from starving. Meanwhile, she followed her own dreams.

You've probably heard of the famous guide and interpreter, especially now that her face graces a U.S. dollar coin. You probably know that Sacagawea was important to the expedition because she knew the territory and languages of the Northwest tribes. But have you ever wondered what she got out of it? Sacagawea knew the explorers were headed to Shoshone territory and she might be reunited with the family and tribe she'd been kidnapped from as a young girl. She also knew she would get to see the distant Pacific Ocean. In fact, both those things happened, and when they did, Sacagawea was very happy.

Sacagawea was born in 1787 into the northern Shoshone tribe, near the Salmon River in present-day Idaho. In Shoshone, her name (pronounced either *Sac-a-ga-WEA-a* or *Sa-CA-ga-wea-a*) means "Bird Woman." During her childhood, Sacagawea and her people lived and hunted in the Great Basin, which stretched through parts of today's Utah, Nevada, Colorado, and Oregon.

SACAGAWEA COIN

WE DON'T KNOW WHAT SACAGAWEA LOOKED LIKE, BUT THE EARLY NINE-TEENTH-CENTURY ARTIST WHO PAINTED THIS LOVELY PORTRAIT CAPTURED HER VISION AND PRIDE.

In 1999, the U.S. Treasury paid tribute to Sacagawea by placing a likeness of her on a golden dollar coin. The image isn't based on any real picture of Sacagawea, though. Clark drew plants, trees, and animals, but never once sketched Sacagawea.

I think it is terrific to have a Native American woman honored this way, but not everyone supported the selection of Sacagawea for the coin. Some people objected strongly, saying that Sacagawea was a victim who was enslaved, married against her will, and forced to work for white men for nothing.

I agree that Sacagawea was treated unfairly, but for this reason she is even more worthy of being honored! First of all, she willingly went on the expedition. Second, she was integral to the explorers' success. Most important, however, Sacagawea's adventurous spirit and determination make her a good representative of American women. At a young age she was wise enough to pick her battles, then stand firm until she won. She also coped courageously with her circumstances.

In Sacagawea's homeland, colossal mountains rimmed grassy plains where vast herds of buffalo roamed. Her tribe depended on buffalo for meat, clothing, and tools, yet so did the Blackfeet and Hidatsa tribes. When Sacagawea was a young girl, those stronger tribes migrated into the basin to hunt and pushed the Shoshone up into the rugged Rocky Mountains.

LEWIS AND CLARK

When President Thomas Jefferson bought a million-square-mile tract of land from France for $15 million (in what was called the Louisiana Purchase), few white men had set foot there. The vast area stretched from the Mississippi to the Rockies, and from the Gulf of Mexico to Canada. In 1804, Jefferson sent Meriwether Lewis and William Clark, a few dozen soldiers, a hunter, and an African American slave named York on an expedition to map and explore the area. Meriwether Lewis was a former captain in the First U.S. Infantry as well as Jefferson's personal secretary. Captain William Clark was a frontier veteran and the younger brother of the famous Revolutionary War hero William Rogers Clark.

The expedition set off in a 55-foot keelboat, *Discovery*, which had a big square sail and 22 oars. Two pirogues, long dugout canoes carved from hollow tree trunks, completed the flotilla. Along with scoping out the landscape, the two men were charged with seeking a navigable water route to the Pacific Ocean and learning about the wildlife (for the fur trade) and the Native Americans of the Northwest.

The expedition took 3 years to complete, and explorers accumulated a wealth of information about the area. When the bedraggled explorers appeared in St. Louis in September 1806, the citizenry called out the brass band to celebrate.

SPELLING SACAGAWEA

Lewis and Clark spelled Sacagawea's name in various ways, including Sahca-gahweah and Sahkah-garwea. In 1814, when their journals were published, the spelling had changed to Sacagawea. Today, some Hidatsa people have suggested her name (which in English means "Bird Woman") should be spelled Sakakawea and pronounced *sä-kä′kä-we-ä*. The Hidatsa say there is no *j* sound in the Hidatsa alphabet, and that *g* is pronounced as a hard *g* (as in get).

Sacagawea, who was descended from a family of honored chiefs, was about 11 when Hidatsa raiders attacked Shoshone camped on the Salmon River. Fleet-footed Hidatsa warriors grabbed Sacagawea and her girlfriend as they tried to flee across the river. A few years later, the Hidatsa sold Sacagawea to Toussaint Charbonneau, a French-Canadian fur trader living with the Mandan tribe. In a Mandan village near present-day Bismarck, North Dakota, she lived with Charbonneau and waited to see what life had in store for her. A year later, that turned out to be Lewis and Clark—and a chance to be reunited with her people.

Sacagawea was 15 and pregnant in October 1804 when Lewis and Clark rowed up the Missouri River to the Mandan village. After 165 days of hard traveling, the exhausted explorers were relieved to find a cordial welcome. In the main Mandan lodge, they puffed on peace pipes and received permission to build a log lodge and stay for the winter. Sacagawea and the others Mandans watched with astonishment as the expedition unpacked. The mountain of food, tents, and firearms amazed her, for the Native Americans traveled light. Sacagawea couldn't understand why the white men needed so many things!

The Mandans fattened up their visitors that winter with corn, beans, and squash from the last harvest. Because her husband spoke French, English, and Mandan, he became a translator between Lewis and Clark and the Mandan. With Charbonneau, Sacagawea spent a lot of time in "Fort Mandan" that winter.

In February 1805, Sacagawea went into labor. After almost two days, the baby still had not arrived. Lewis and Clark, who had grown fond of Sacagawea, were worried. They asked Charbonneau if his wife would live. "Don't worry!" the trader told the explorers. "The women just gave her dried rattlesnake to hasten the birth." Ten minutes later, sure enough, a baby boy greeted the world and was named Jean Baptiste. Captain Clark grew especially fond of the baby and nicknamed him Pomp. Later, he'd even name a rock formation in Montana after the boy—Pompey's Pillar.

As the winter drew to an end, Lewis and Clark asked Charbonneau to be their guide on the rest of the journey. Sacagawea overheard and piped up, "I want to go, too." The thought of taking Sacagawea gave the explorers pause. After all, as a woman she belonged at home, sweeping up the wigwam. Not only that, she'd have 2-month-old Baptiste in tow. But Lewis and Clark talked it over and realized that Sacagawea would be a great asset. After all, she spoke several native languages, most importantly, Shoshone. The explorers would pass right through Shoshone land and hoped to buy fresh horses from them. Also, having a woman along might convince the tribes they would encounter that their mission was a peaceful one. The pros outweighed the cons, so in April 1805 Sacagawea joined the trek.

During the journey, Sacagawea proved even more useful than the explorers had predicted. "Janey," as Clark nicknamed her, rose from her blanket at dawn and nursed her son. Then she strapped him to her back, gathered fresh water for the camp, and prepared meals of buffalo, antelope, or deer flavored with edible plants, roots, nuts, and berries. Each evening, after marching up and down hills for 12 hours, she did it all over again.

Lewis and Clark probably took all this "women's work" for granted, but they sure realized how invaluable Sacagawea was after she rescued their precious journals and equipment. On a wild stretch of river a supply boat carrying Sacagawea, Charbonneau, and the gear tipped over. Fearing for his life (he couldn't swim), Charbonneau held onto the canoe. Meanwhile, Sacagawea calmly held onto Pomp, balanced herself on the back of the canoe, and gathered the cargo floating in the churning water! Captain Lewis was so moved by Sacagawea's swift thinking and bravery that he named a stream Bird Woman's River in her honor.

Sacagawea was both bright and unflappable, but she was as excited as a kid on Christmas morning when in late August 1805 she finally found her family and tribe! The group came to a place near the headwaters of the Missouri. Sacagawea began to jump up and down. "It is a camp of my people, the Shoshone!" she shouted. Sure enough, the group soon met up with the Shoshone chief, Cameahwait, and 60 warriors. When Sacagawea set eyes on them, she began to madly suck her fingers (a sign of true joy). "My people, my brother!" she cried while dashing up to the startled Chief Cameahwait. Sacagawea gave him a big bear hug as she explained in Shoshone, "It is Sacagawea, your sister who was lost!" Cameahwait

returned the embrace, and much to Lewis and Clark's surprise, the warriors began hugging the crew, too. "We were all caressed and besmeared with grease and paint, until I was heartily tired of the national hug," the somewhat stuffy Lewis wrote.

After the hug fest, the group stayed a while in the Shoshone village. The Shoshone warned that the route to the Pacific was difficult. It was far too late in the season, they explained, to take canoes and supplies over the mountains to the navigable Columbia. But Lewis and Clark were determined to push on despite the obstacles. They bought 29 fresh horses from the Shoshone and kept on trekking toward the Pacific.

Perhaps Sacagawea wanted to stay with her long-lost tribe; perhaps she wanted to push on and see the ocean. We'll never know, for Lewis and Clark didn't comment on her feelings or thoughts. But willingly or unwillingly, Sacagawea joined the expedition on its arduous trek through the Bitterroot Mountain Range on the LoLo Trail and on wild rides on the Clearwater, Snake, and Columbia Rivers. It was late November by the time the explorers reached the Pacific Ocean and set up winter quarters.

In the first coastal camp, the party nearly froze to death from frigid winds and rain. The explorers convened a meeting to discuss the wisdom of relocating. For some reason, the move was controversial enough to require a vote. And guess whose voted was counted with the men's? Way before American women won the right to vote, Sacagawea did just that.

Although their new quarters were warmer, it was a lean and miserable winter. Game was scarce and the local Clatsop tribe wasn't thrilled enough with the party's presence to share. When the food supply had dwindled to a few crumbs and bones, Clark fell ill. Sacagawea took pity on him and gave him a hunk of hard bread she had squirreled away for Baptiste in case of an emergency. On another hungry day, the men learned that a whale had washed up on the beach a few miles away, and they started out to harvest some blubber. Sacagawea hollered, "Wait for me! I'm coming, too." The men waved her back to the camp, but Sacagawea planted her feet in front of her employers and demanded: "Have I not helped you come all this way? Have I not given you bread saved for my child? Do I not deserve to see the giant fish?" The explorers hurriedly agreed that Sacagawea was more than welcome!

In March 1806, the group began their long trip back to the Mandan village. Only one major mishap occurred when Lewis and some men off on a separate excursion were attacked by several Blackfeet warriors, but they managed to escape and return to the rest of the group. Lewis and Clark had been right. Sacagawea's presence had convinced the northwestern tribes that the explorers were on a mission of peace. In fact, the only time any member of the party was bothered was when Sacagawea was not around.

After 2 years and 8,000 miles, Lewis and Clark returned east as heroes. Before they said goodbye to their guides, they paid Charbonneau $500. There was nothing in the budget to pay Sacagawea, though, so Clark offered another kind of assistance. "Let me take Pomp to St. Louis to raise and educate," Clark said. Sacagawea thought this would be a fine opportunity for her son, but he was a little young to be leaving his mother at age 2! She agreed to send him when he was a bit older, and she did.

We know little about Sacagawea's life after the Expedition. Even the date of her death wasn't known for a long time, and is still disputed. In 1812, records show that at a Missouri River trading post a Shoshone wife of Charbonneau gave birth to a daughter, Lisette, then died shortly afterward. People assumed this was Sacagawea, but it turned out that Charbonneau had actually married two Shoshone women. So it might have been the other wife who died, not Sacagawea. A woman on the Wind

River Reservation in Wyoming Territory who died in 1884 claimed that she was Sacagawea.

Long after Sacagawea's adventures, writers and historians began to tell her life story based on what was in Lewis and Clark's published journals. It was nice that she got some attention, but she sure was stereotyped. Native American women have long been portrayed in one of two ways—as noble Indian princesses who helped whites, or as dirty primitives who lived like animals. Sacagawea, like Pocahontas, became a well-known "Indian princess." She was famous because she helped some very important white men complete a historic exploration.

I think it's about time we celebrate Sacagawea for who she was: a strong, generous, determined woman with an adventurous spirit . . . a woman who knew her own mind and walked her own path with pride and dignity.

SACAGAWEA'S CHILDREN

After Sacagawea's reported death in 1812, William Clark took permanent custody of Jean Baptiste and Lisette. No records remain about Lisette, so she may have died young.

Jean Baptiste learned to be a proper white gentleman, then gave in to an adventurous spirit much akin to his mother's. At age 19, he made friends with a young German prince and returned with him to Europe. For 6 years, he flitted about, seeing the sights and hobnobbing with royalty, but his original home eventually called to him. Pomp left the palaces of Europe to become a trapper and guide in the same wilderness he'd passed through as a papoose on his mother's back.

Gertrudis Barcelo

(1 8 ? ? - 1 8 5 2)

Under three different dominions—Spain, Mexico, and the United States—a beautiful, black-eyed gambling queen of Santa Fe kept her wits about her and lined her pockets with gold. La Doña Maria Gertrudis Barcelo was called La Tules, a Spanish nickname for Gertrude.

Although her early years are cloaked in mystery, Gertrudis was born around 1800, in Spanish-controlled Mexico. Her parents, well-to-do Spanish ranchers from near Sonora, made sure Gertrudis learned to read, write, dance, sing, and otherwise charm the world. Few whites (called Anglos by Spanish speakers) would have crossed her path, for the Spanish viewed Americans as the enemy. However, Mexico gained independence from Spain in 1821, and big changes were in store for Gertrudis.

Two years later, in 1823, she married an upper-class Spanish don (*don* means "sir" or "noble" in Spanish). Together they moved north to

"POKER ALICE"

It was common for women to gamble on the frontier, and they came from all walks of life. "Poker Alice" Ivers shed her upper-crust English ways and plied her trade in saloons all over the west. It was the promise of fortune that had lured Alice's family to the gold mines of Colorado. In the boomtown of Leadville, she married a successful mining engineer, Frank Duffield, and played poker only for sport. After her husband died, however, she got serious. She gambled for a living in the saloon owned by Frank Ford, the man who shot Jesse James. When a man threatened her dealer friend, W. G. Tubbs, with a knife, Alice shot and killed him. Tubbs was so grateful to Alice for coming to his rescue that he married her! Alice's husbands had a way of dying on her, though. When W.G. died, Alice loaded his corpse onto a wagon and drove 50 miles through a blinding blizzard to see him buried properly. After that, Alice survived yet another husband, then fell happily into saloon keeping until her death in 1930.

the sleepy frontier village of Santa Fe. Not much is known about her husband, Manuel Antonio Sisneros. Documents from that time don't often mention him. In fact, La Tules didn't even take her husband's name and bought property on her own. She was determined to hold onto her independence!

The town of Santa Fe had been around for a couple of centuries when Gertrudis arrived. The mission and *presidio* (fort) built by the Spaniards in 1610 still stood. Surrounding the village were cattle ranches, as well as Sioux, Arickara, and Comanche villages. La Tules was smart and knew that Santa Fe would not remain a sleepy village for long—

fortunes would be made by those who stood ready to seize opportunity.

With her husband, La Tules opened a hotel. The adobe walls kept the heat in during the chilly winters and out in the dry, hot summers. Santos—carved images of saints—graced the walls. From craftsmen and nuns at the mission, La Tules bought furnishings and items made of wood, tin, iron, silver, linen, and fine lace. The foothills of the majestic Sangre de Cristo Mountains loomed in the distance.

The hotel did a brisk business. Under Spanish rule, U.S. traders and settlers were kept from the provinces, but Mexico opened the door wide. In fact, Mexico even offered free land in what they called Nuevo Mexico (New Mexico) to any American who swore allegiance to Mexico and converted to Catholicism. Thousands accepted this offer. On the 1,000-mile Santa Fe Trail, ox- and mule-drawn caravans hauled men, women, and children to Santa Fe and points west. Some died at the hands of Sioux and Arickara warriors unhappy with the swarm of newcomers.

La Tules welcomed the multitudes to her little hotel. Due to her booming business, she closed this small place and opened a grander one on the central plaza, with a lavish first-floor casino. This time, the property deed had only La Tules's name on it—not her husband's. In fact,

THE SANTA FE TRAIL FOSTERED TRADE BETWEEN THE UNITED STATES AND MEXICO.

from this time on, Manuel is rarely mentioned in historical records, so he may have moved away. Eventually, 60 Santa Fe casinos would compete for customers, but La Tules didn't worry. Hands down, hers was the big enchilada! Along with other budding Mexican and Anglo tycoons, La Tules grew rich catering to an amazing hodgepodge of people— señoritas of the Spanish upper classes,

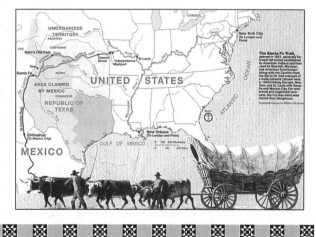

15

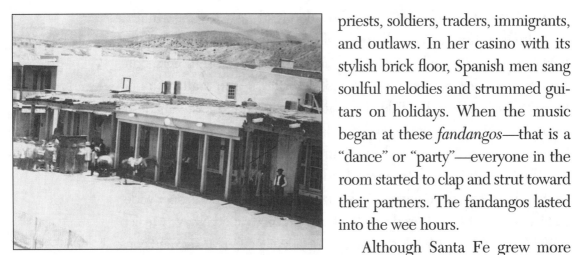

priests, soldiers, traders, immigrants, and outlaws. In her casino with its stylish brick floor, Spanish men sang soulful melodies and strummed guitars on holidays. When the music began at these *fandangos*—that is a "dance" or "party"—everyone in the room started to clap and strut toward their partners. The fandangos lasted into the wee hours.

Although Santa Fe grew more culturally segregated, especially after America gained control of the Southwest in 1848, that didn't hold true in La Tules's gambling parlor. There, race, ethnic background, and sex mattered far less than how much gold people laid on the table.

La Tules's gambling parlor was on the central plaza, just down the street from the Spanish-built Palace of the Governors. At a green table divided into four squares, she dealt hands of *monte.* The Spanish card game, which means "mountain," was played with a deck of 40 ultra-thin cards. Four suits represented four parts of the world: America, Asia, Europe, and Africa. Dealers were typically men, but La Tules owned her own shop! She called the shots.

La Tules's poker face and swift hands were legendary. When she swept through the room with a long, large gold cross dangling around her neck and a lace *rebozo* (shawl) draped over her shoulders, her patrons looked up from their cards. The elegant establishment raised the eyebrows of first-time visitors, too. It boasted thick carpets imported from Brussels and a mahogany bar with great mirrors behind it. Ornate chandeliers were lit with hundreds of candles. Bright light was a must in the casino, for barmaids and dealers had to watch constantly for cheaters and angry losers. Each of La Tules's employees wore a hand-tooled leather holster, where a little pistol called a derringer rested. If a customer got out of hand, watch out!

La Tules's main casino was the haunt of men of all backgrounds, as well as Mexican women (and a few Anglo American women who didn't turn up their noses at gambling). But only an elite group of men were welcome in private rooms behind thick walnut doors. Of course, La Tules was allowed because it was her place. Among the elite were professional gamblers, as well as top Mexican and U.S. officials and military officers. These high rollers played for big bucks and bouncers enforced strict rules. The back rooms were rife with deal making as well as gambling. When the bigwigs negotiated land and trade deals, La Tules got in on the action. She soon became one of Santa Fe's largest landowners.

By staying on the good side of powerful men, La Tules became a power to be reckoned with herself. She had a chance to wield that power when America began scheming to obtain New Mexico. She obtained information about each side's movements and passed it on for money. At first, La Tules was unsure of who would win control of New Mexico—the United States or Mexico—so she kept on the good side of both.

By August 1846, however, La Tules had cast her lot with the Americans. They outnumbered the Mexicans but desperately needed provisions, and La Tules decided to help. She sent a message to the American commander, General Stephen Kearney, and offered to loan him money. He gladly took the money, which helped turn the tide in America's favor.

In the end, the Americans marched victoriously into Santa Fe—and guess where they headed first? To La Tules's casino! "Doña Barcelo," an officer announced to her with a flourish. "We are here to escort you to a victory ball!" La Tules joyfully complied and danced the night away with General Kearney and his American officers.

By 1948, Mexico had lost its grip on Texas, California, Arizona, and New Mexico. Then gold was discovered in nearby California and Colorado. Again, Anglo American settlers descended like a swarm of locusts, but this time most wanted to wipe out all traces of the Spanish culture. This put a damper on La Tules's business, yet when she died in 1852 she was still a wealthy woman.

On her deathbed, Doña La Tules told the Catholic bishop of Santa Fe that she wanted "a funeral fit for a queen." The bishop, who inherited much of her fortune since she left no heirs, was delighted to honor her wishes. Sixteen hundred dollars bought an ornate casket that was drawn by several fine steeds, and a distinguished gravestone paid fitting tribute to the one and only gambling queen of Santa Fe.

WOMEN IN THE MILITARY

Long before women could legally join the military, some found ways to serve. Only snippets of information about their lives can be gleaned from official government documents. One of those women, Elizabeth Newcume, fought in the Mexican-American War. She disguised herself as a man and served at Fort Leavenworth. After 10 months, she was discovered and discharged. Later, Congress awarded her 160 acres for her service.

Sarah Borginis worked as a cook for the army at Fort Texas. She didn't pretend to be a man, but when Mexican troops in Matamoros bombarded the fort, General Zachary Taylor issued her a musket and gave her the rank of colonel. She went on to own hotels in El Paso, Texas, and Yuma, Arizona. After her death in 1866, the army buried her with full military honors.

Narcissa Whitman

(1 8 0 8 - 1 8 4 7)

Fur traders who crossed the country on the Oregon Trail with Narcissa Whitman were captivated by her lively gray eyes and ready smile. They lent her the biggest horse to ford deep rivers and brought her sweet wild berries. For these buckskin-clad traders, women were a novelty. Narcissa and her friend Eliza Spalding were the first two white women to cross the frontier on the Oregon Trail.

In 1808, Narcissa Prentiss was born in Prattsburg, New York. As the oldest daughter among eight siblings, Narcissa helped raise the younger children and run the family farm. Nevertheless, the family valued education and made sure she went to school. She attended Franklin Academy and a teacher's training school in Troy, New York. Narcissa then taught for a while, but deep down she nurtured another dream.

NARCISSA HAD TO BE MARRIED TO REALIZE HER DREAM OF BEING A MISSIONARY.

One of the most exciting jobs recently opened to women was missionary work among non-Christian peoples around the world. Narcissa longed to save souls in India, Africa, or some other exotic foreign land—and maybe ride an elephant or camel, too. However, her application to the missionary board was declined. The posts were only offered to married women working with their husbands.

Narcissa could have solved that problem by marrying a fellow student and would-be missionary, Henry Spalding. But when he proposed, Narcissa turned him down flat because she thought he was too full of himself. The angry young man thought golden-haired Narcissa had a lot of gall turning down such a fine catch.

In 1836, Narcissa met Marcus Whitman, who had been assigned to start a mission among the Cayuse tribe of the Pacific Northwest. He and Narcissa discussed their mutual passion for missionary work and decided to marry. At the wedding, Narcissa's mother and sisters cried. Narcissa, however, was dry-eyed and excited. She cut off locks of her golden hair and gave them to her sisters and female friends. She promised to write. Then she and Marcus left New York forever.

The mission board had a surprise in store for Narcissa, though. For the journey across the Oregon Trail, the newlyweds were paired with another newlywed couple assigned to work with the Nez Percé in Idaho. After traveling to Missouri by sleigh, barge, and riverboat, the Whitmans met up with the jilted Reverend Henry Spalding and his new wife, Eliza! Narcissa soon loved Eliza like a sister, but she and the still-annoyed Henry gave each other the cold shoulder for the entire trip.

Narcissa and her party began their overland journey outfitted with several mules and cows, two wagons, and a couple dozen horses. For safety, they traveled with a wagon train of 70 male fur traders. On the prairies, Narcissa was happy. She loved buffalo meat and didn't mind

cooking using dung for fuel. She sprang from her
bed at daybreak when the wagon train cap-
tains called: "Arise! Arise!" and the mules
started braying. After a quick breakfast,
the same voices called, "Catch up!
Catch up!" the signal to mount and
move. From 6 A.M. to 6 P.M., the train
snaked forward to the next camp. "I've
never felt so healthy and happy my entire
life," Narcissa wrote.

CHORES SUCH AS
FEEDING THE
MENFOLK FILLED
NARCISSA'S DAYS
ON THE TRAIL.

When the plains turned to peaks, some of
the romance wore off. The zigzag roads upset the
wagons, and river crossings threatened to drown horses, wagons, and people. But each day Narcissa grew more daring, and she had
no regrets. "I would not go back for the world," she wrote in her diary.
"I am hungry and weary, yet contented and happy. I long for rest, yet do
not murmur."

Near the end of the journey, the Whitmans stopped to rest a while
at a trading post on the Columbia River. Narcissa was overwhelmed by
the beauty of the sun dipping behind two snowcapped peaks—Mount
Hood and Mount St. Helen. The traders at the post were pleased to
have two female guests. At a lavish dinner, they toasted Narcissa and
Eliza, then served up roast duck, fresh salmon, and apples. After five
months of wild game and corn cakes, Narcissa's mouth watered. The
apples, Narcissa was astounded to learn, were grown from seed that an
English ship captain had carried across the ocean in his pocket.

Reluctantly leaving the post behind, the party headed for Fort Walla
Walla, in a valley tucked between the Cascade and the Rocky mountains. There the Spaldings left for Idaho to live among the Nez Percé,

THE WHITMAN ROUTE

and the Whitmans climbed aboard a boat manned by six oarsmen. For several miles, they glided over water smooth as glass to reach the Wai-ilatpu (pronounced *Why-ee-lat-poo*) mission site. When Narcissa climbed out of the boat, a group of Cayuse women gathered around, chattering happily and kissing her cheeks.

With such a warm welcome, it's no wonder that at first Narcissa was overjoyed by the Cayuse people and excited about the future. Before long, an adobe and log home, a church, and a large garden graced the peninsula on the Walla Walla River. Narcissa only took a few days off to give birth to a healthy baby named Alice.

At their mission, Marcus began to hold church services and practice medicine. Meanwhile, Narcissa ran the household and taught in the mission school. Cayuse attendance at church and school was excellent, which pleased Narcissa to no end. Yet the honeymoon period among the Cayuse only lasted a few short years.

On a Sunday morning after church services, Narcissa was dealt a heavy blow. Little Alice wandered off and drowned in the river. Narcissa took the gray dress she'd worn on the wagon train and sewed Alice a shroud. After the burial, Narcissa fell into a deep depression.

While Narcissa grieved, the public back east learned that Narcissa and Eliza had survived their Oregon Trail experience. Suddenly, hundreds of women felt safe to make the journey. In 1843, Marcus returned east to lead an expedition of a thousand settlers back to Oregon.

The immigration ushered in a new phase in Narcissa's life. She spent far more time assisting white settlers than befriending the Cayuse. For Narcissa personally, the arrival of the settlers seemed like a godsend. Orphaned children of deceased pioneers made their way to her door and filled the void left by Alice's death. Narcissa adopted several of the

WOMAN TEACHERS

Narcissa Whitman was one of many teachers on the frontier. Catherine Beecher wrote a book titled *The Duty of American Women to Their Country*, which inspired many single women to join the profession and head west. In the mid-1850s, Protestant and Catholic churches, as well as organizations such as the National Popular Education Board, sent hundreds of young female teachers west.

In the 1850s, Lizzie Ordway—who jokingly called herself Bachelor Bess—came to Oregon to teach. Later, she ran for the elected post of Kitsap County superintendent of schools. The *Seattle Post-Intelligencer* wrote: "It may be a good joke to put a woman in nomination, but I do not regard the office of school superintendent of so little importance as to vote for a woman at the polls." The public did not agree with the newspaper, though. In 1881, Lizzie beat her male opponent and got the job.

children, as well as several others born to area fur traders and their Native American wives.

The orphans had lucked into a good thing, too, for Narcissa was a dynamite mother. She took her children on woodland picnics and berry-picking hikes. She taught them all about plants and trees and rock formations. She gave each a garden plot of his or her own and sang them to sleep in a sweet soprano voice. She oversaw weekly baths and regular chores. Once again, Narcissa's spirit soared.

Helping immigrants get settled and mothering her brood meant that Narcissa and her husband were doing far less with and for the Cayuse, however. The missionary couple was too involved elsewhere to realize how much the Cayuse resented the growing white presence. They reacted by rejecting the Whitmans' Christianity. (Some Cayuse were wooed away by the Catholic missionaries, who wisely allowed traditional dances and songs to be part of church rituals.) This made Narcissa angry and impatient. She told the Cayuse that if they didn't attend church and give up their heathen ways, they'd burn in hell.

As you can imagine, the Cayuse grew tired of being told they were sinners. The cultural divide grew even wider after 1846, when Britain and the United States decided who owned what territory in the Pacific Northwest. The two nations divided the Oregon country, and thousands more whites descended. The settlers built cabins on Cayuse land, shot their game, and even shot at them! Then an 1847 smallpox epidemic brought by white settlers killed half the Cayuse tribe. (Far fewer whites died, for their bodies had greater immunity to the smallpox virus.)

The smallpox deaths were the last straw for the grieving and angry Cayuse. On November 29, 1847, Chief Tiloukaikt and a band of Cayuse warriors launched a surprise attack on the mission. In a bloody raid that dragged on for hours, Cayuse warriors burned the mission to the ground

THE FATE OF THE CAYUSE

What happened after the raid is a common story when it comes to warfare between native peoples and whites. The raid escalated into a war, and the outnumbered, outgunned Cayuse ultimately lost. Tiloukaikt and other warriors who had attacked the mission realized their entire tribe was nearly exterminated. To save the remaining few, they surrendered and were sentenced to hang. Chief Tiloukaikt did not go silently, however. On the gallows he told the watching crowd: "Did not your missionaries teach us that Christ died to save his people? So we die to save our people." In 1855, the Cayuse, Umatilla, and Walla Walla tribes ceded 6.4 million acres to the United States. In exchange, the tribe was "given" the Umatilla Indian Reservation, today comprised of 172,000 acres. The Whitman Mission is now a national landmark.

and killed 14 people. Narcissa hadn't seen it coming and was devastated to discover how much the Cayuse had grown to despise her and her husband. It was too late to remedy that, but Narcissa courageously tried to save as many people as possible before she was killed herself.

In fact, Narcissa's personal strength emerged during the raid. She herded women and children into hiding under floorboards and in attics. She tried and failed to save her husband's life. She nursed the wounded and tried in vain to negotiate with the warriors. Thanks in part to her courage, the mission women and children were spared. Because she was considered a top leader among the whites, she, too, became a victim of the warriors' tomahawks.

Juana Briones

(1 8 0 2 – 1 8 8 9)

A s a child raised in Branciforte, a pueblo village next to a Spanish mission in California, Juana Briones learned to be submissive and obedient—and careful. Her father, Marcos Briones, was a soldier stationed at the Santa Cruz mission overlooking the shimmering Monterey Bay. Juana didn't go to school, for there was none. But every day she went to church at the mission, where silver-framed pictures of saints adorned the adobe walls and gold-plated chalices graced the altar.

THE SANTA CRUZ MISSION IN 1856.

Life wasn't a picnic for those inside or outside the mission walls in Spanish California. The *padres* (priests) ruled with iron fists, using shackles, lashes, and stocks on their disobedient or slow-moving subjects. Among these subjects were soldiers and their families, as well as Native Americans who'd been rounded up and brought to the mission to be forcibly "converted" to Catholicism. In this culture, women were considered property that husbands and fathers could treat however they liked. But Juana's submissiveness did not last forever. She went on to become an independent, wealthy, and generous landowner.

When she was a teenager, Juana moved with her family to the Mission Dolores, near Yerba Buena, which later was renamed San Francisco. Juana was of marriageable age, and most of the eligible men around were members of the Spanish cavalry. Although there were respectable men among the soldiers, many were rough characters. Two

ISLAND OF THE BLUE DOLPHINS

One remarkable Native American woman of the Chumash tribe who evaded capture by the Spanish lived on San Nicholas Island off the California coast. When her people were rounded up by Spanish soldiers in the early 1800s, the young woman jumped from the boat carrying her away from her island home. She swam to shore through currents so treacherous that the soldiers decided not to return for her.

Everyone assumed that the lost woman had perished alone on the island. But 18 years later, hunters found her living quite well in a tidy little hut. Thinking that she could see her tribe and family again, she went to the mainland with them. At the Santa Barbara mission, the astounded padres took her in and baptized her Juana Maria. She soon discovered that all of her people had died of diseases brought by the Spaniards. There was no one left who spoke her language. No one knew her name. Seven weeks later, she died, too. A beautiful, award-winning novel, *Island of the Blue Dolphins*, is based on her story.

hundred soldiers lived in barracks surrounded by a 12-foot adobe wall. Many dressed in rags, were fond of drink, and bullied the natives. One favorite pastime was hunting, shooting, and branding Native American Christian converts. In fact, the padres had more problems with the calvary than with the supposed "savages." Some had been sent to California because they had committed a crime of desertion, mutiny, theft, or even murder.

From these ranks came Juana's husband, Apolinario Miranda. Chances are good that the marriage was arranged by the padres and Juana's family. In 1820, a year before Mexico became independent from Spain, the pair were married. A year later, independent Mexico split up the large Spanish grants and gave plots to favored individuals. Juana and her husband settled on some of her father's land outside the mission, but soon moved closer to the harbor in Yerba Buena. After Mexico gained independence from Spain, foreign trade boomed, and Juana knew that meant opportunity galore.

During her marriage, Juana gave birth to eight children. In addition to running their busy household, Juana supported the family economically by engaging in trade. Because her husband had a serious drinking problem, he wasn't much of a rancher or businessman, so Juana sold milk and beef to the crews of Russian, American, and Spanish ships that docked in the bay. She also harbored sailors who jumped ship because they wanted to remain in California, ran a busy tavern, and nursed the sick. Sailors with scurvy, women delivering babies, children with broken jaws—Juana treated them all. She also added to her own brood by taking in five orphans from New Zealand!

Juana's achievements were accomplished alone and against great odds. Her soldier husband not only drank too much, he also beat her.

Divorce was not an option because it was hard to obtain in civil courts and illegal in the eyes of the Catholic Church. Juana complained to military authorities about Apolinario's abuse. They did nothing. At last, in 1836, Juana could not take it anymore. She left her husband and moved her brood to a house just below today's Telegraph Hill, which came to be called La Playa de Juana Briones.

Juana's husband, however, wouldn't let matters be. He tried to force her to return home, but Juana refused. She asked the justice of the peace to order her husband to stay away. The justice obliged, then seized some of Apolinario's property when he didn't obey the order.

Property was at the heart of the next step taken by 42-year-old Juana in 1847. Because they were still legally married, her husband could sell the family land. To prevent that, Juana visited the chief lawman, the Catholic bishop. She asked for a legal, church-approved separation. She told the bishop, "My husband did not earn our money. I did. My husband does not support the family. I do." Only legal recognition of Juana's status as an independent woman would allow her to retain ownership of the

THE 1849 GOLD RUSH TRANSFORMED SAN FRANCISCO FROM A SLEEPY VILLAGE INTO A BUSTLING CITY.

land and money she had acquired over the years. The bishop had great respect for Juana and little fondness for her no-good man. The separation was granted, and Juana was free.

The newly liberated señora continued to do a brisk business and lead a lively social life. Traders from Boston exchanged manufactured goods for Juana's cowhides (called California banknotes). European and American guests attended parties at Juana's home during carnival and festival times. Juana's lively daughters, who liked to play games of catch with confetti-filled eggs, drew a bevy of suitors.

In 1846, great changes shook California. The United States wrested California from Mexico, and two years later gold was discovered in Sutter's Mill. Hispanics and Native Americans were soon vastly outnumbered by Anglo Americans. Yerba Buena, renamed San Francisco, became a teeming city practically overnight.

Juana wasn't bothered by the U.S. coup at all. In fact, when her Anglo friends suggested she become an American citizen, she did. But when gold drew 30,000 fortune seekers, Juana moved to a 1,400-acre ranch she owned in the Santa Clara Valley. Ranching, not city life, was Juana's dream, so she settled on Rancho La Purisima Conception.

The Briones family ranch was a home, social hall, and hospital all rolled into one. Anglos, Hispanics, and Native Americans came for bear fights, calf roping, and pig roasts. The place teemed with a dozen dogs and children of all sizes, ages, and races. Sick people also came to recuperate under Juana's watchful gaze. When one of her nephews who helped her with the nursing later became a full-fledged doctor, Juana was deeply proud.

Yet being Spanish in American California could be risky, and Juana easily could have lost everything, like so many other Spanish Californians did. In 1852, the U.S. government sent a letter to Juana saying her lands would be seized. The reason? Her husband had died! Juana's legal separation was not recognized by the authorities. By then, Juana had a great deal to lose. Along with the Santa Clara ranch, Juana also owned property near San Francisco and elsewhere.

Juana, a shrewd businesswoman, dug out years of written contracts, maps, and business dealings related to her lands and her marriage. Then, for 12 long years, she fought the U.S. government in court. It took a hearing before the U.S. Supreme Court to settle the case. But Juana's tenacity and determination paid off. She held onto her land until her death in 1890 and became a legend among Californians.

Part Two

THE AGE OF SETTLEMENT
(1840S-1870S)

THE MID-NINETEENTH CENTURY *brought a flood of migration to the frontier, mostly by whites, but also by a small number of African Americans escaping from slavery and post–Civil War strife in the South. In territories such as Missouri and Kansas, ruffians associated with the Confederacy or Union formed violent rival gangs and vied for political control.*

More than 300,000 people traveled on the Oregon Trail alone, and 10,000 of those died from accidents or sickness. The majority of settlers bypassed the midwestern plains and prairies because so few trees grew there that they believed the soil was barren. Also, many feared Native Americans (some displaced from the East) who lived in and roamed through the area. Instead of the plains and prairies, land seekers headed for the Far West, Southwest, and Northwest. Gold and silver in those areas drew fortune seekers and entrepreneurs.

Meanwhile, Utah's unappealing desert beckoned Mormons seeking freedom from harassment, and Kansas drew both pro- and anti-slavery forces who were determined to force the territory to adopt their position—or die trying.

Everywhere, Native Americans struggled against the occupation of their land.

Luzena Stanley Wilson

(1 8 2 1 - 1 8 ? ?)

When news that gold had been found in California hit Missouri in the spring of 1849, Mason Wilson told his young wife, "I'm bound for California, Luzena. You stay home, and I'll send for you later." As fast as you can say Jumpin' Jehosophat, Luzena nipped that plan in the bud. The 28-year-old told her husband, who was about 14 years her senior, "Where you go, I go, Mason, with my two toddling babes in arms."

Luzena and her husband were small farmers with little to lose—or pack. It only took a few days to give away most of their belongings. It took less time to gather 3-year-old Thomas, 1-year-old Jay, the old milk cow, and their pair of mules. They hitched the mules to a covered wagon and one morning before dawn they joined a small train of six wagons. In June 1849, the family ferried across the wide Missouri that night and lit their first campfire in what Luzena called "an unbroken, unnamed wasteland that stretched to the Pacific." The Wilsons were bound for the gold fields of California, like nearly 50,000 other adventurous souls. Of that multitude, only a couple hundred were women!

That first night, Luzena wondered if she'd made a huge mistake when 200 Native Americans visited their camp. They were friendly enough, but Luzena clutched her children so tight that they whimpered in pain. Because there was safety in greater numbers, Luzena insisted that her husband ask the Independence Company, camped nearby, if their family could join the much larger wagon train. Mason returned to inform Luzena that the company flew colorful banners and had a brass band—but it didn't have women and children. "We don't want to be slowed down by bothersome females," the gold-seeking men had told Mason.

That peeved Luzena to no end! The group's insulting answer roused her courage, and her fears died a sudden death. Luzena was so angry that she even sent a message to the Independence Company. "I am only a woman," she wrote. "But I am going to California, too—and without your help!" With their lively mules, the Wilson family soon left the Independence Company and its slow oxen in the dust.

Luzena's excitement abated as well as her fear, for monotony took hold. Day after day, the same weary routine was performed of harnessing and unharnessing the mules and cooking meager rations over a fire of sagebrush and scrub oak. Crossing the South Platte River, with its quicksand riverbed, shook up the tedium quickly enough, though. The Wilsons' wagon made it to the other side, but the team behind stopped in midstream. The frantic driver whipped the frightened animals until their hides were raw. But slowly they sank into the soft quicksand bottom and disappeared beneath the surface. The man made it to shore, but without a possession to his name.

In her diary, Luzena recorded such dramatic incidents, as well as

LUZENA GREW
WEARY, BUT
SOAKED UP THE
BEAUTY OF THE
LANDSCAPE AND
THRIVED.

descriptions of the magnificent scenery. Rather than the wasteland she expected, Luzena discovered a pristine land. She found it breathtaking, despite the dunkings in rivers, overturned wagons, and funerals where the only singing was done by the wind, owls, and coyotes. Graves marked with simple stones lined the trail; so did belongings tossed out to lighten the load. For Luzena that included three precious sides of bacon and a dirty calico apron. Such mutual suffering led Luzena to develop binding ties to the men with whom she traveled. "Any man among us," Luzena wrote, "would protect me and my children with his life."

After three dusty months on the Oregon Trail, the Wilsons came to an 80-mile stretch through the Utah desert. During the night, the temperature dropped below freezing. By day, nearly unbearable temperatures above 100 degrees fried their skin, parched their tongues, and scorched their feet through the soles of their shoes. Dust hung like a cloud in the air, reddening their eyes. Skeletons of oxen and mules that had died in the struggle lined the trail, and sun-bleached human bones were scattered among broken-down wagons.

Because they were well prepared, the Wilsons made it through the desert. Days later, they learned that the Independence Company had suffered far more on its journey. Two of its members staggered into the Wilsons' camp nearly dead from hunger and thirst. The bootless, hatless, tattered men told the Wilsons that several of their party had died in the desert. The rest had turned around and returned to Missouri. As Luzena gave them food and drink, they begged her forgiveness for their earlier haughtiness.

By September, the Wilsons were 50 miles from their Sacramento destination. A well-dressed man in a new white shirt stopped for a little conversation and Luzena suddenly realized that her skirt was frayed, her gloveless hands were callused and brown, and her shoes were worn

DEATH VALLEY DAYS

Luzena and her family trudged across the northern desert and Rockies, but Juliette Brier and her family took the southern route—the Old Spanish (or Santa Fe) Trail. They hoped to avoid the pitfalls and dangers of the northern route. Along the way, they heard of a shortcut, and with some brazen young men from Illinois, they decided to try it out. In early November, they crossed a desert they named Death Valley and got hopelessly lost. Juliette, the young men suggested, should just give up and wait. They'd forge on ahead and send back help. Juliette knew that giving up would mean a shallow grave in the sand! "I have never kept the company waiting, nor have my children," she told the men. "Every step I take will be toward California." Then Juliette walked 100 miles with one child on her back and another in her arms. She also had to help her weakened husband, who lost 100 pounds. Like other pioneers, the Briers learned there simply was no easy path through the wild frontier.

through. "It revived in me a spark of womanly vanity," Luzena wrote. "I drew my ragged bonnet over my sunburned face and shrank from his gaze." Soon, however, Luzena learned that the 99-percent-male population of California could give a hoot about her appearance. She was a woman—a reminder of mothers, sisters, and daughters left behind—and was therefore precious to the lonely men.

That very same night, Luzena got an inkling of the value of a woman in the mining camps—especially a woman who could cook! A gold miner offered to pay Luzena for some fresh-baked biscuits. When she placed the steaming bread in his gnarled hand, he laid a gleaming five-dollar gold piece in hers. As he stared down at the biscuits, the miner muttered, "You know, I'd give twice that for bread baked by a woman."

When the Wilsons reached the tent city of Sacramento, Luzena discovered her gold piece had been lost. But the Wilsons were young, strong, and hopeful. All around them, gold seekers played cards, drank whisky, fed their teams, and traded trail stories. Word quickly spread that a woman with children had arrived, and dozens stopped by just to get a look at them.

BECAUSE WOMEN WERE A RARE SIGHT IN MINING CAMPS, MEN TENDED TO GAWK.

The next morning, the aroma of Luzena's wonderful cooking soon brought men who wanted more than just to gawk. They came to her fire and asked for breakfast. For a plate of eggs, bacon, and coffee, each man forked over five dollars' worth of gold dust—and an enterprise was born.

In Sacramento, a store, stone bank, and ramshackle hotel were the only permanent structures among a

sea of makeshift tents and muddy paths. Every day, hundreds of wagons and pack mules passed by laden with picks, shovels, rubber boots, and provisions. Schooners and sloops anchored at the riverbank to unload more gold seekers who'd made the trip by sea. A gaunt, unshaven town crier on a Mexican pony rode through town clanging his bell, announcing the time, a mail call, or a show at the local theater. Such pastimes were more common than the shootings, gambling, and theft that came later with a rougher crowd.

The Wilsons' goal was to eventually make enough money to buy land and farm. Gold mining, they wisely believed, was too unpredictable. Instead, they'd hoped to cater to miners with gold dust burning holes in their pockets. However, when Luzena went to the store for food and cooking supplies, she discovered outrageous prices, wormy flour, and sour milk. Yet Luzena worked with what she had, making her customers their meals and pocketing her slim profits. She got some satisfaction in hearing the men swear that her dishes were fit for kings.

Luzena and her husband scraped together some cash by selling their oxen and wagon and selling Luzena's meals. It's not clear what her husband was doing to earn money while Luzena cooked, but he may have worked as a laborer. With their nest egg, they bought an interest in the town hotel and moved there.

Luzena's first impression of that dump haunted her dreams for the rest of her life! Dripping candles were jammed into old whisky bottles. Filthy bunks lined the walls on either side of the long room. At a bar lined with dusty bottles and glasses, a few miners sat hunched over their whisky. In one corner, a man scratched out a tune on a fiddle. In another, a young man cried as he read a letter from home.

Luzena strapped on her apron and got to work—dusting, scrubbing, and cooking for a motley crowd that gathered daily at her table. When she presented food, the swearing and fighting stopped. Forlorn gazes of lonely, homesick men followed her every move. When she smiled, they showered her with adoration. After several weeks, however, Luzena found it hard to smile back. From sunrise to sundown, the work never ended, and she had no time to gossip or listen to men's troubles. The worst part, though, was lying in bed at night, too tired to get up and offer care or

LOTTA CRABTREE

Every mining camp had a theater, even if it was a big arbor of wild grape vines fitted with a canvas curtain! In the 1850s, little Charlotte "Lotta" Crabtree sang and danced and played her banjo in many of those theaters. Lotta grew up in a gold-mining camp and began performing in the makeshift theaters when she was only 7. The redhead's appreciative audience threw her gold nuggets—and a star was born. Lotta's mother tucked nuggets and coins into her apron pocket. With her protective mother by her side, Lotta performed throughout the frontier. By 1864, the crude little towns of the West had lost her to larger stages in New York and Chicago. Lotta also traded in her own act for roles in real plays such as Harriet Beecher Stowe's *Uncle Tom's Cabin*. Lotta invested her earnings wisely in stocks and bonds. When she died in 1924, she left

REDHEADED LOTTA CRABTREE GOT HER START SINGING AND DANCING IN MINING CAMPS AND FRONTIER TOWNS.

a fortune of $4 million. Since Lotta had no children, her money went to charities supporting aging actors, veterans, and animals.

prayers for sick men dying in their bunks. Diseases, such as scurvy, dysentery, and Panama fever ran rampant in dirty, crowded Sacramento.

After only a couple of months, the work took its toll on Luzena and she, too, fell ill. The Wilsons decided to sell their interest in the hotel and return to the tent city until Luzena regained her health.

In those early days of the California gold rush, the population of Sacramento ebbed and flowed like the sea. There might be 1,000 to 10,000 residents on any given day. Luzena's tent was no finer than those around her, but she tried to make it like home. While her bachelor neighbors ate sitting on the ground, Luzena, her husband, and her guests dined at a table and chairs fashioned from wooden packing boxes and boards. Having finer furnishings didn't make sense, even if they could have afforded them, for the tent wasn't waterproof. When it rained everything was soaked through and the floor became a muddy swamp.

Luzena's first Christmas in the camp was a memorable one. She was cooking supper and the men were coming home from work when the crier's bell clanged. As he galloped past, Luzena heard him call, "The levee's broke!" Her husband ran with the rest to rebuild the earthen dam that kept the river from flooding the town.

While the men tried to shore the dam back up, Luzena awaited news. No one came, and then a knee-high flood of water rushed into the tent. Luzena snatched up the children and headed for high ground. By midnight, the water reached the second story of the hotel, where Luzena, her children, and a dozen others had taken refuge. Cries for help echoed from every direction. Luzena's husband and others manned rafts and boats, following the voices, trying to rescue the stranded.

Luzena watched the walls of the stone bank collapse into the rushing waters. Waves dashed against the rickety hotel, making it shake and creak. In their makeshift attic home, lawyers, miners, mechanics, and merchants tried to distract Luzena's boys with stories and songs. For 17 days, the group survived on food pulled from the passing water. When the flood receded, Luzena told her husband, "I've had enough—let's head for Nevada City!"

Sacramento was buzzing about how miners had struck gold in Nevada City, but the Wilsons were without animals or a wagon to make the trip. A neighbor offered to take the family, a stove, and two sacks of flour for $700. Luzena almost cried, and the man took pity on her. "I'll take you all, ma'am," he said, "if you'll pay me back someday." Luzena swore he'd have the first $700 they earned, and off they went.

It took 12 days to slog their way through the 60 miles of snow-covered mountains and muddy ravines to Nevada City. (Once on a hillside of pure ice, the oxen stiffened their legs and the wagon slid straight down for a quarter of a mile!) Like Sacramento, the camp was a tent city that lined two deep gulches. In the streams, brawny miners wielded picks and shovels or stood in icy water, washing soil away from flakes of gold. Frenzied men scurried about so intent upon their work that they scarcely took time to breathe.

Tentless and penniless, the resourceful Wilsons built a shelter with pine branches. While Luzena's husband went in search of saplings to strengthen the structure, she set to work rebuilding the family's finances. She bought two boards and built a table. On credit, she bought food at the store. One night when Luzena's husband came back from the mountain with the saplings, he found 20 miners devouring meals at Luzena's table. After each man finished, he rose, thanked Luzena, and paid her a dollar. Luzena Wilson called her "restaurant" El Dorado, after the fabled Mexican city of gold.

From the first day, Luzena's restaurant was a smash hit. The Nevada City mines—dubbed Coyote Diggings—netted gold galore. Everyone had money, and everybody spent it. "Business is so good I took my husband into partnership," she wrote to friends back in Missouri. In only six weeks, Luzena had saved enough money to proudly repay the $700 to the fellow who had brought them from Sacramento. Several weeks later, the pine shelter was replaced with a frame home, then with a hotel that slept a hundred men a night. Luzena hired waiters, cooks, and chambermaids to staff her growing domain.

Among Luzena's guests were several professional gamblers who popped in and out of town for a game with miners suddenly rolling in dough. Tempers often flared when the card sharks "fleeced the suckers," cleaning out their newly full pockets. The crime rate in Nevada City soared.

One night, when her husband was away on business, Luzena had a real scare. She had just put her children to bed and was resting her feet by the hotel kitchen fire. Suddenly, she heard a pounding at the door and voices crying, "Burn the hotel! Burn it down!" Luzena rushed to the front door, threw it open, and confronted a sea of angry faces.

"Search for him," someone shouted and tried to push past her.

"No, no; burn him out," cried another.

Terrified, Luzena tried to shut the door as voices cried, "Let us in! Burn it down! Let us in!"

"What do you mean? What do you want?" Luzena replied, holding back the crowd.

Confronted with Luzena's determined refusal to let them in, the men finally calmed down enough to explain what they wanted. A gambler who had killed a man named Tom Collins was staying in the hotel and they wanted to search for him. "Well, men," Luzena replied, "come in and search, but no more of this talk about burning!" The search was fruitless, and years later Luzena learned why. When she was a gray-haired old woman, the gambler visited and confessed to Luzena that he knew the mob had been after him that night. "I stood in the crowd in disguise," he said. "I felt bad that you were frightened, but if I had come forward, they'd have hanged me for sure."

After six months, Luzena and her husband had $20,000 invested in the hotel and ran an unofficial bank. At one time, Luzena had more than $200,000 in gold in a hotel that had no lock, let alone a safe! It never occurred to her that it might be stolen. Life seemed great, but after only 18 months in Nevada City hard times hit again. Instead of a flood, this time it was a fire.

One night, calls of "Fire, fire!" woke the Wilsons in the nick of time. The hotel—and most of the growing town—was on fire. Bells clanged and gongs sounded to rouse the sleeping people. The tents, pine houses, and hotel ignited with a spark, and the blaze was unstoppable. More than 8,000 residents were homeless and penniless—all their money sunk into the buildings, goods, and gold dust reduced to ashes. Overnight, the Wilsons' fortune went from tens of thousands of dollars to $500 that Luzena's husband had in his pockets.

Although Nevada City was rebuilt quickly, the town had lost its appeal for the Wilsons. In truth, they were heartily sick of boomtowns that were a flash in the pan for a little while, only to be wiped out by flood or fire. They decided that despite their empty pockets, they'd somehow obtain a piece of land to call their own.

The Wilsons wandered the low-lying hills south of Sacramento until they discovered a valley with a spring-fed stream. Here, by a well-traveled road, under a spreading oak, the Wilsons decided they would stay forever. They had no property deed or money. But that didn't stop them. Like many pioneers, they became squatters, hoping that if they improved the land, whoever owned it would sell it to them in the end.

Hay was selling in San Francisco at $150 a ton, so Luzena's husband got to work making hay in the meadow. Luzena set up her stove and hung out a shingle that read Wilsons' Hotel. Boards from the wagon bed became a table; stumps and logs became chairs. Before long, several guests a day tethered their horses and retired to the haystack to sleep. The next morning, they paid $1 for their spot on the haystack and another for their breakfast.

After her first summer in Vaca Valley, Luzena went visiting. She saddled a horse, hiked her two boys up behind her, and rode 12 miles to the nearest neighbors, the Wolfskills. The neighbors owned 50,000 acres of prime land, bought from Señor Vaca, owner of a large Spanish grant. Señor Vaca also owned the land on which Luzena and her husband camped. Naturally, Luzena was eager to befriend the Spaniard, and did. Before long, the Wilsons had a legal deed to 700 acres—a nice piece in the Vaca Valley.

Nothing, however, came easy on the frontier. The California land commissioners in San Francisco were reviewing, and often rejecting, Spanish people's claims to land. The commission decided the Spaniard who had sold the property to the Wilsons had not legally owned it. Instead, they ruled that the state owned it and could sell it to land speculators, who would then resell it to new settlers.

As the news of the commission's ruling spread, land speculators descended like hungry wolves and hired armed thugs to scare the Wilsons away. But the Wilsons stood their ground. Luzena's livid husband told the thugs that his family would keep their land or clobber every man who tried to take it away. The Wilsons waged a legal battle for 12 years, and finally won title to their land.

Meanwhile, Luzena decided she liked making money with her own business and built another hotel. While she ran it, she had two more children. Concerned about her children's education, Luzena also started a school, which later grew into Pacific Methodist College. As if that wasn't enough to keep her busy, she also became the community's de facto doctor. A medicine chest a customer gave her in payment for a bill had launched her new career!

Year after year, Luzena ran her hotel and watched the area turn from frontier backwater into a thriving agricultural valley covered in vineyards that produced California wines. One by one, the old-time frontier settlers passed away, and eventually Luzena joined them. The exact date of Luzena's death is unknown. However, it was after 1881, for that is when her daughter recorded the story of Luzena's adventures in a book called *Luzena Stanley Wilson: '49er Memories Recalled Years Later for Her Daughter, Correnah Wilson Wright.* This woman of the California gold rush and ace entrepreneur weathered some wicked storms and emerged the stronger for it. Under a clear California sky, she nurtured her dreams—and didn't rest until she'd made them come true.

CHAPTER 6

Eliza Snow

(1804–1887)

ELIZA SNOW ENCOURAGED MORMON WOMEN TO EDUCATE THEMSELVES AND BETTER THE COMMUNITY.

Eliza Snow became a leader of the best-organized expedition to cross the American frontier. She married the top two leaders of the Mormon Church, helped turn a dismal Utah desert into a lush "promised land" despite many dangers, and published nine volumes of poetry and an autobiography.

Born in Becket, Massachusetts, in 1804, Eliza moved with her family at age 4 to the forested plains of Ohio. In a frontier school, she wrote a school assignment in verse, impressing her teacher with her literary talents.

Oliver and Rosetta Snow, Eliza's parents, were pals with Alexander Campbell, a religious scholar who founded the Campbellite sect. Later, the group's name was changed to the Disciples of Christ. Campbell convinced Eliza and her siblings that established churches had strayed from

JOSEPH SMITH

Joseph Smith, founder of the Mormon Church, said that in 1827 an angel named Moroni appeared before him. Moroni, the son of Mormon, said God had chosen Joseph to translate a book of golden plates buried near Joseph's home in Palmyra, New York. The plates had been compiled in the fourth century by his father, Moroni said.

Joseph Smith claimed that he and Moroni dug up the book and spent three years translating it into English. The book, Smith said, told the story of Jewish people who came from the Middle East to the Americas before the time of Christ. Native Americans were the descendants of these surviving Jewish tribes. The book also instructed Mormons to live according to ancient traditions and to open themselves to the Holy Spirit. During worship ceremonies, Mormons possessed by the spirit fell into trances, danced wildly, and spoke in an ancient language or "tongue."

Such claims and beliefs were pretty hard for other Christians to swallow. In fact, many found Mormonism downright blasphemous. In New York, Ohio, Missouri, and Illinois, the Mormons were beaten, tarred and feathered, burned out of their homes, and driven out of town.

the laws laid down in the New Testament. Massive numbers of Protestants, Alexander Campbell believed, would desert established denominations and flock to his "one true church."

Most of the Snow family did not, however, stick with Joseph Campbell for long. Eliza and her siblings were wooed away by Joseph Smith, a former Campbellite who had formed his own religious group called the

Church of Latter Day Saints. (Other people called them the Mormons.) Joseph claimed he was a true prophet, just as Christ had been. God sent him visions and told him to teach the true word of God, he said.

In her mid-20s, Eliza began attending Smith's church in Kirtland, Ohio, and felt a "deep spiritual awakening." She was excited to find a religion headed by a living prophet, and was drawn to the message that ordinary people, including women, could be "filled with the Holy Spirit." Joseph Smith's teaching that women should be as educated as well as men made Eliza's hungry mind soar. "Seek ye out of the best books words of wisdom," Joseph preached—and Eliza rejoiced.

In 1835, 31-year-old Eliza officially joined the Mormon "Saints," in Kirkland. Because she was so well read, Joseph Smith asked Eliza to teach his children, and she jumped at the chance. In the household of the prophet, the pair grew very close. They took long walks together in the evenings and talked for hours about religious matters and the Mormons' tribulations.

Eliza gave her heart to Mormonism and began penning Mormon hymns. "Zion's poetess" wrote: "I will smile at the rage of the tempest, and ride triumphantly across the boisterous ocean of circumstance." The Saints sang Eliza's words and took heart.

In 1841, after seven years in Ohio, Eliza and the Mormons fled with lynch mobs hot on their heels. The Illinois state legislature welcomed the Mormons to Nauvoo, Illinois, and Eliza hoped that the Saints had at last found a permanent home.

In Nauvoo, the Mormons swiftly became a powerful force. Joseph Smith became the mayor, commanding general of the militia, and a newspaper editor. The Mormons ran highly successful businesses and farms in and around Nauvoo.

The Mormons also welcomed 10,000 Morman converts to town. The religion grew like wildfire, especially among the European poor. To help the bedraggled and penniless converts, Eliza and Emma Smith (Joseph's wife) founded the Female Relief Society of Nauvoo. The elite group of women gained unheard-of status, and Joseph Smith was their biggest fan. He threw himself into teaching the women organizational skills: how to run meetings, hold civilized debates, and conduct elections. "They learn much more quickly than men and make fine democrats!" Smith boasted proudly. Along with helping the poor, the women kept the children in line. "If you correct them," Smith confided, "you'll save me the trouble." In a single year, the women's society grew from 20 women to 1,100.

The elevation of women gave the Mormons' enemies more to dislike about Mormonism, as did Joseph Smith's announcement that God had commanded him and other Mormon men to take multiple wives. Smith proclaimed, "The Lord commanded the people of ancient Israel to take plural wives, so has he ordered us. To obey this command will bring eternal joy in the heaven and help us replenish the earth."

Emma Smith, Joseph's wife, wasn't too thrilled about this, to say the least. In fact, she was more than a little upset when she found out that her husband had actually taken other wives secretly for several years. In the end, Joseph married between 20 and 50 women (accounts vary). Most of his wives were half his age—except Eliza, who was in her late 30s in June 1842, when she also became "sealed to the chosen-one."

Throughout her life, Eliza maintained she never regretted her marriage to Smith. That was brave talk, for being one of Smith's wives could be a harrowing experience. When the news about polygamy among the Mormons got out in Illinois, for example, Joseph Smith's days were numbered. The non-Mormon newspaper railed against the Saints, and some Mormon guerillas responded by trashing the printing press. Joseph and his brother, Hyrum, ended up in jail, and a mob of a hundred armed non-Mormons smeared their faces with mud and stormed the jail. From the doorway, a man fatally shot Joseph Smith in the chest and collarbone. His final words as he fell to the ground were "O Lord, my God!"

After the shooting, the Mormon Church was split in two. One faction, led by Emma Smith and later Joseph Smith Jr., stayed put in Iowa. Eventually, they became the anti-polygamy Reorganized Church of Jesus Christ of Latter Day Saints. Eliza, however, joined the faction led by Brigham Young, which headed to Utah and founded Salt Lake City. On a scouting mission to find the Saints a new home, Brigham Young reported seeing a spirit of light hovering over a sterile sea and desert. The exodus of 70,000 Mormons to that "promised land" began.

MORE THAN 70,000 MORMONS MIGRATED TO SALT LAKE CITY IN THE 1800S.

Two years after the mob killed Joseph Smith, in 1844, Eliza married his successor as head of the church, Brigham Young. He left for Salt Lake City in one wagon train, and she followed in another. Before saying goodbye to friends and climbing into her covered wagon, Eliza used some of her few coins to buy a bottle of ink. With it she would write songs, letters, and personal journal entries during the trek.

At night, when the moving village of 300 wagons pulled into small circles, Eliza wrote in her journal about crossing swift rivers and black muck that reached the tops of the wagon wheels. Yet rather than being weary, Eliza was invigorated. She laughed over the antics of a captured baby eagle and wolves that approached the camp at night. Unlike the "gentiles" (non-Mormons), the Mormons revered wildlife and only killed what they could eat. (In fact, Mormons believed in conservation long before it was popular.)

Eliza's wagon train followed the murky, shallow Platte River for 600 miles. Pioneers warned the Mormons: "The Platte is a mile wide, six inches deep, too thick to drink, too thin to plow, and maybe a pretty good river if it didn't flow upside down." The Mormons camped on sandy beaches and washed off trail dust. They held daily services, too, when Eliza often "received the gift of talking in tongues." This energized her to no end. In fact, with each passing mile, the ladylike Eliza grew more robust. In the beginning, she rode in a covered wagon. Within weeks, however, a whip in her hand and wide-brimmed bonnet tied securely under her chin, she drove a wagon through sleet, dust, hail, and snow.

On the first leg of the journey, tensions mounted as Mormons and non-Mormons competed for water and grazing ground. Yet an amazing thing began to happen. On the frontier, mutual need helped ease the tensions between the former mortal enemies. The Mormons were expert ferry builders, and the non-Mormons had extra flour and cornmeal. A friendly trade of river crossings for food soon healed some angry wounds. Eliza saw this as a sign from God that the Mormons were, indeed, on a righteous path.

The path led Eliza and her group over the Rocky Mountains on the route traveled by the doomed Donner party the year before. High willow bushes, thorny roses, and birch forests tore the wagon cover to

THE DONNER PARTY

The Donner party of 1846–1847 wasn't the first to cross the Sierra Nevada on the Truckee Trail (named for the grandfather of Sarah Winnemucca's grandfather, whom you'll meet in Chapter 11), yet it certainly is the most famous and tragic. The Donner party of 87 people included 17 women and 43 children. Although they started out early enough in the spring, a shortcut through the Utah desert weakened them and depleted their supplies. An early winter storm then descended before they could get through the mountains.

At Truckee Lake, they huddled together in three cabins and some structures cobbled together from tents, buffalo hides, and brush. At first, the Donner party members hoped for a break in the weather; later, they prayed for rescue. But across the mountains, people merely assumed the settlers had plenty of cattle to slaughter and eat. They didn't know the severity of the storm or that the cattle had wandered into the woods and been buried in snow drifts.

The weakened settlers ate boiled leather, dogs, and mice—and eventually the bodies of their dead family members and friends. On December 15, the first settler died, and in the end 44 perished. In desperation, a few small groups set off through the snow-covered mountains, but only 7 people made it—2 men and 5 women. Only when the 7 staggered into civilization were rescue parties hastily organized. Conditions were so terrible, though, that even some of the rescuers died trying to save the Donner party.

Survivor Virginia Reed Murphy was only 12 that horrible winter, but years later she wrote a heartrending memoir of the ordeal and the dramatic rescue of the survivors. You might like to read the book, which is titled *Across the Plains in the Donner Party*.

shreds, but at last they came to an over-
look above their new home. Blue peaks
surrounded a vast desert, in the center
of which shimmered a gray-blue lake.
The Mormons had reached their promised land. Unable to contain herself,
Eliza shouted out her joy: "Hosannah,
Hosannah, Hosannah!"

In the center of the vast 200,000-
square-mile Salt Lake Valley was the
shimmering, landlocked, 250-square-
mile Salt Lake. All the salts and dissolved
minerals remained in the lake water,
instead of being washed into the sea.
Spain, Mexico, France, England, and the
United States had ignored this "wasteland," but the Mormons built homes and

fences from stones pulled from the rocky soil and built irrigation ditches
that watered the barren fields. With hard work and determination, the
Mormons accomplished what no one believed they could. From a desert,
they made a garden.

FORTY-THREE
DONNER PARTY
SETTLERS
PERISHED IN
THE SIERRA
NEVADA.

By 1860, Salt Lake City was a growing city of homes, stores, mills, and
banks. Because she was a wife of Brigham Young, Eliza had a particularly
fine stone house with a trellised veranda. Down the street, she shopped
for leather boots, cotton dresses, and woolen blankets. The women's
group, which she now headed, helped found a social hall and school.
Eliza was determined that Salt Lake City would be a place where wages
were high, sickness was rare, and crime was unheard of—and it was.

The Mormons of Salt Lake were doing so well that Eliza spearheaded an effort to bring in new converts. Mostly immigrants from Britain and Scandinavia, these folks were too poor to afford even a wagon. Three thousand Mormons pulled and pushed wooden carts across the frontier to Salt Lake City between 1856 and 1860.

With no children of her own to raise, Eliza threw herself into her leadership role. The highest position a Mormon woman could hold was president of the Relief Society, and Eliza didn't hesitate to exert influence. In new Mormon communities throughout the frontier, she preached that women and men were equally responsible for the public good. Critics derided her, but Eliza didn't care. She encouraged women to start social centers and open stores to sell their home produce—milk, butter, eggs, yarn, and clothing. She helped women attend medical schools and urged them to write for the newspapers. Under Eliza's influence, a group of women even started their own newspaper, the *Woman's Exponent*. The paper—and Eliza—campaigned successfully for women's suffrage in Utah, which was granted in 1870.

Eliza remained active and energetic until her death in 1887. She founded a hospital and wrote nine books, including poetry, history, and children's books. "If we put our minds to it," Eliza told her Mormon sisters, "there is no limit to what we can accomplish."

Bridget "Biddy" Mason

(1 8 1 8 - 1 8 9 1)

Bridget "Biddy" Mason, born a slave in 1818, claimed her freedom and found opportunity on the American frontier. In 1891, she died a rich and free woman who had stared adversity in the face—and had come out swinging.

When Biddy was young, she was the property of Robert and Rebecca Smith, plantation owners in Georgia or Mississippi. In 1847, the Smiths became Mormon converts and left for Salt Lake City, Utah, with slaves in tow. Four years later, the Smiths brought their slaves with them to southern California. Among them were Biddy and her three daughters, Ellen, Ann, and Harriet. (Biddy may have been married, or Smith may have fathered the children. No one knows for sure.)

IN 1860, BIDDY GOT A CERTIFIED COPY OF THE JUDGE'S ORDER THAT DECLARED HER FREE.

Biddy and her children traveled with a wagon train, but they didn't ride. Instead, they walked mile after mile, herding their owner's sheep. Biddy arrived in Los Angeles and learned that California had recently joined the Union as a free state. That meant slavery was prohibited, yet Biddy and her family remained enslaved for five more years. When officials at last began enforcing the California law, Smith hastily made secret plans to move Biddy, her sister, Hannah, and their 11 children to Texas, which permitted slavery.

Biddy wasn't about to let that happen, though. On the sly, she visited a free black man who owned a successful livery stable. Charles Owens was a leader among a dozen free blacks living in Los Angeles, then a small town of 1,600. The free blacks had bought or been given their freedom and settled in California after it was admitted to the Union as a free state in 1850.

Although slavery was illegal in California, blacks were far from equal. Most held low-wage jobs, including being laundresses and maids. Blacks (and Native Americans) could not testify against whites in criminal or civil court. They could, however, file lawsuits and be present in court, which was a good thing for Biddy.

Biddy had some pull with Owens, whose son was in love with Biddy's teenage daughter Ellen. To save his son's girlfriend and her family, Charles got busy thwarting Smith's flight. Charles Owens contacted his friend—the sheriff! "Smith's been keeping slaves for five years, and he's sneaking them out through the Santa Monica Mountains tonight," Owens told the sheriff. "It's time to act!" That night, the sheriff and his deputies swooped down on Smith's wagons and rescued Biddy, Hannah, and their 11 children.

The case to determine what should happen to Biddy and her family went to court in 1856. In court, Biddy's owner claimed that he was merely a transient passing through California with his slaves, which the law allowed. Biddy could easily have refuted that, but could not testify against Smith in court. Thankfully, the judge was sympathetic. He called Biddy into his chambers and let her speak on her own behalf.

JULIA LOVEJOY

From 1854 into the 1860s, the slavery issue drew immigrants to Kansas, not gold or grain or glory. An 1854 law had made it the right of territories to vote over whether slavery would be permitted within their borders. Abolitionists made it their business to populate Kansas to ensure it would be slavery-free; pro-slavery forces did the same thing to ensure that slavery would be allowed. Along with settlers, both sides sent money—and lots of guns.

In 1855, Julia Louisa Lovejoy of New Hampshire arrived in Kansas with her family to serve the anti-slavery cause. She reported on developments there for New England newspapers. During the mob violence and guerilla warfare that followed, Julia never stopped writing, even though she lost her daughter to smallpox, had all her belongings stolen, and was forced to flee from her home by a pro-slavery mob!

In the end, Kansas joined the Civil War as a free state, but the violence continued before and during the Civil War. Julia reported on friends tortured and shot before her eyes, yet nothing shook her belief in the abolition of slavery. "Kansas must be redeemed and saved, and we want a hand in helping that happen," she wrote.

After the war, when things had calmed down a bit, the Lovejoys stayed in Kansas to farm. In her spare time, Julia spoke out for women's suffrage. Seeing firsthand the results of inequality and hatred in Kansas, she explained, had convinced her that equality should extend to females: "Once I hated the idea of women politicians, but no true woman could be in Kansas and not be enthusiastic about universal freedom for all."

"I've been kept in slavery against my will in California, and slavery is not allowed here," Biddy said firmly. "I want to be free." The judge listened, nodded, then returned to his bench in the courtroom. There he banged his gavel and proclaimed, "Biddy Mason, you and your family are free from the shackles of slavery, in the great state of California."

Biddy and her family hugged and cried and rejoiced. Then Biddy rented a house and began working as a midwife and nurse. Biddy settled in Los Angeles, where Dr. John Strother Griffin hired her, and she was soon in high demand among his pregnant patients. Biddy also worked as a nurse for prisoners in the county jail and patients in the county hospital. During a smallpox epidemic, she risked her own life nursing the sick.

With her earnings, Biddy bought two lots just outside of town on Spring Street, then two more. The lots became prime downtown real estate that was worth a fortune.

Making a good living wasn't Biddy's main goal in life, though. Her house on Spring Street became a shelter for stranded ex-slaves and travelers in need. Long lines of poor people of all races found a helping hand at "Grandma Mason's" home. After local flooding wiped out area homes, she opened grocery store accounts for the victims, then paid the bills. There was no end to Biddy's generosity, for her philosophy was "If you hold your

ROSE JACKSON

State and territorial laws governing slavery contradicted each other right and left and led to some dangerous situations. Like Biddy Mason, Rose Jackson headed to the frontier in 1848 with the family that owned her. The Allens had planned to leave Rose behind because Oregon law made it illegal to bring in slaves. But the daughters of the family begged their father to let Rose come, so they smuggled her all the way across the country in a box with air holes drilled in it! At night, Rose was let out to stretch her legs and breathe the fresh night air. In Oregon, Rose was eventually freed, married John Jackson, a stagecoach groom, and raised two children.

hand closed, nothing good can come in. But the open hand is blessed, for it gives in abundance, even as it receives."

In addition to helping those in need, Biddy worked to strengthen the black community. The First African Methodist Episcopal Church was founded in her living room, and with black organizations founded in the 1860s she worked against discriminatory laws. Many of these organizations still exist today, such as the National Association for the Advancement of Colored People (NAACP).

After Biddy's death in 1891, her children and grandchildren became business and civic leaders in the African American community. A century later, her courage, generosity, and leadership were recognized publicly when the mayor of Los Angeles declared November 16 to be Biddy Mason Day. Today, at Biddy Mason Park near the site of her Spring Street home, a colorful mural honors Biddy's legacy as a powerful black woman who never gave up and never stopped giving.

Charlie Parkhurst

(1 8 1 2 - 1 8 7 9)

One-eyed Charlie Parkhurst, one of the best stagecoach drivers on the frontier, was a skinny fellow with sun-baked skin. A black patch covered one eye, and a nasty scar ran across one cheekbone. With callused hands, the stagecoach driver kept a six-horse team hugging hairpin curves on treacherous mountain roads.

But Charlie Parkhurst was no ordinary driver. The "whip," as drivers were called, harbored a huge secret. Charlie wasn't the "he" everyone thought. To the surprise of all who had known him, Charlie turned out to be . . . Charlotte!

It was a splendid disguise—that's for sure. Charlie's bachelor roommate never guessed, nor did the godson to whom she left her estate. No one discovered the truth until she was laid out for burial on the day she died.

Charlotte Parkhurst was born in New Hampshire in 1812. Either an uncle raised her, or she grew up in a Massachusetts orphanage.

Whichever it was, chances are good that she did not have an idyllic childhood. In her midteens, Charlotte ran away, chopped off her brown hair, stole a boy's clothing—and became Charlie.

In Vermont, then Iowa, no one discovered Charlie's secret. She found work at a few livery stables, feeding and grooming horses. After a while, she learned to ride and drive a team. Before long, Charlie was a master teamster who handled teams of four and six like an old pro. Horses were Charlie's friends and family. She loved them, and they knew it.

Charlie applied for a job with the Overland Stage line. Legend has it that several men vied for the job Charlie wanted. The owner created a pop quiz for the applicants. "How close could you allow the stage to get to a thousand-foot drop and be sure the passengers would be safe?" he asked. The other would-be whips shouted out, "Five feet!" "Two feet, six inches!" And so on. But Charlie muttered in her low growl: "I'd keep that stage as far away from the edge as possible." That was the right answer, and Charlie was hired.

Charlie wasn't a friendly sort or a handsome fellow. In fact, she rarely spoke or looked directly at folks. After a horse kicked and blinded her, she wore a black patch over one eye. The patch earned her the nickname "One-Eyed Charlie." Being a whip took great concentration, a tough

PASSAGE TO CALIFORNIA

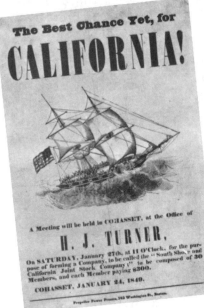

Between April 1849 and January 1850, 40,000 people sailed by ship from eastern port cities, around Cape Horn to the Pacific coast. It was a long, hard, dangerous journey. Ships' advertisements misled passengers, so few were prepared for six months at sea. Sickness, storms, wormy flour, and foul water made it a truly hellacious experience. And that's not even mentioning the ones that didn't make it—shipwrecks were common!

THE SHIPBOARD JOURNEY TO CALIFORNIA WAS AS TOUGH AS OVERLAND TRAVEL.

skin, quick reflexes, and a bit of a wild streak. Charlie had all that, which made her popular with stage owners. They liked it even more that Charlie didn't drink.

For three years, Charlie worked in Iowa, then the wide-open spaces and lonely routes in California lured her west. By ship, via Panama, she landed in Santa Cruz.

There, Charlie found work easily—and kept at it for 20 years. She ran the Sand Hill Station for the Wells Fargo Stagecoach Company on the Santa Cruz-Los Gatos Road. Her 20-passenger Concord coach was drawn by six gorgeous mustangs. When careening down the narrow roads at full speed, the coach rocked like a ship on a wind-tossed sea. The stage had no horn, so Charlie used the standard whip technique to warn oncoming traffic. She stuck two fingers in her mouth and blasted a shrill whistle before each curve!

The station where Charlie hung her hat was just a shack with a stable attached. Her life was as rough as any cowboy's on the range, which suited her just fine. She lived alone, bathed alone (when she did bathe, which was rarely), and at night she bedded down in the hay by her horses. There was no way that anyone would think this tough fellow who chewed tobacco, hollered at horses, and strong-armed highwaymen was a woman!

Highwaymen were a big problem along the stagecoach lines, so Charlie learned to shoot and drove with a rifle by her side. But it's hard to hold the reins of six galloping horses and aim a gun. That's why an outlaw named Sugarfoot (because he wore cloth made from old sugar sacks wrapped around his feet) had no problem robbing Charlie's stage during one run. Charlie was no fool. With a shotgun pointed at her face, she threw down the strongbox that held the passengers' jewels and cash. However, as Sugarfoot galloped away, Charlie swore she would get revenge. The next time Charlie encountered Sugarfoot, he was dead before he could raise his rifle.

Charlie was only in her 50s when rheumatism stopped her driving career in its tracks. But Charlie didn't hunker down in a rocking chair. Work was second nature to her, so she took up saloon keeping, cattle ranching, and chicken farming. Along the way, she joined the Odd Fellows Association (little did they know she was the oddest fellow of all) and found a business partner: another grizzled old bachelor named Frank Woodward.

The pair was rooming together on Election Day in 1868, when Charlie traveled to town to vote. Unbeknownst to the poll workers, Charlie became the first woman to vote, a year before any territory or

ANNIE OAKLEY

Charlie had to be a good shot as a stagecoach whip. But no shooter could hold a candle to Annie Oakley. Her name, of course, screams out frontier heroine! Yet Annie didn't grow up on the frontier or live on the frontier. Instead, she was a showbiz likeness of the real McCoy, which was fast fading away as the twentieth century dawned. Annie was a dynamite representative of frontier women, though: independent, hardy, and talented.

AS A *WILD WEST SHOW* STAR, ANNIE OAKLEY DREW HUGE CROWDS.

Annie, who was actually born Phoebe Moses in 1860, could shoot a bull's-eye by age 8, and to help her Ohio farm family she shot and sold game to a Cincinnati hotel. Her talents led to her showbiz career when she beat a professional sharpshooter, Frank Butler, in an amateur shooting match. After she beat him, they fell in love!

Phoebe married Frank, took the stage name of Annie Oakley, and hit the road. Because she was the big draw, Frank hung up his six-shooters and managed her career. In 1884, Annie joined *Buffalo Bill's Wild West Show* and stayed for 16 years. As the real American frontier grew tamer by the day, the *Wild West Show* took a nostalgic nation by storm. With Wild Bill Hickock, Sitting Bull, and other former frontiersmen, she kept the romance (minus the gritty reality) alive.

Annie Oakley really was a darn good shooter, as well as an actress. Across America and Europe, Annie shot cigarettes out of Frank's mouth and shot spinning dimes in the air. She leaped over a table, grabbed her rifle, and shot a bullet through the center of a playing card from 30 yards away. She shot the head off a running quail and the cigar out of a German kaiser's mouth! She competed in the male world of sharpshooting, and earned her nickname, "Little Sure Shot."

state gave women that right—and five decades before women won the vote nationwide!

In 1879, Charlie's tobacco chewing caught up with her, and she died of mouth cancer. In her will, Charlie left an estate worth $600 to 12-year-old George Harmon, a neighbor boy who had helped care for her during her last days.

Even in death, Charlie's real identity would have remained a secret if her wishes had been followed. Charlie had told friends she wanted to be buried in her grubby everyday clothes. But the women of the area insisted on cleaning and dressing up the body before burial. Naturally, they got the surprise of their lives! A doctor was called in to certify the obvious truth that Charlie was a woman. He examined the body and said, "Yep, he's a she all right."

Reaction to the news was mixed. Reporters from all over the country gleefully told the tale. Local folks were mostly stunned. But Frank, Charlie's roommate, was livid! He swore a blue streak that he'd been so deceived by the fellow he'd shared a buffalo-hide blanket with many a time. He also wondered about whether he should doubt the identity of his new partner, "Curly Bill"!

Part Three

THE AGE OF EXPANSION

(1870S–1900)

FROM THE 1870S *to the early 1900s, railroads increased the pace of settlement and commerce. Cattle ranching empires were established in parts of Texas, Montana, and Colorado. New discoveries of gold, silver, copper, and lead attracted fortune seekers to Arizona, Dakota, Montana, and Alaska (bought from the Russians in 1867). Wealth from the cattle ranching and mining created boomtowns that also attracted rustlers, thieves, and murderers. The Calvary and many Native American tribes still battled over land and policy. Popular literature idealized and romanticized the frontier, which drew more nonconformists and free spirits. Pioneer farmers discovered the prairies were fertile, built houses of sod, grew grain, and prospered. As the physical frontier disappeared, bold frontier women fought their way into male-dominated fields such as medicine, law, and journalism. Territories and states west of the Mississippi were the first to give women the vote.*

Martha "Calamity Jane" Cannary

(1 8 ? ? - 1 9 0 3)

I n the early 1860s, teenage Martha Jane Cannary (sometimes spelled Canary) was eager to move from Princeton, Missouri, to Virginia City, Montana, a shantytown of miners, outlaws, and vigilantes. She was plunging headfirst into adventure—and trouble. During most of the 5-month wagon-train journey to Virginia City, Martha Jane didn't ride with her mother and the other women and girls. No sunbonnet with a six-inch brim shaded her face to keep it milky white. This girl was determined to join the boys and men on horseback, and no amount of lecturing stopped her.

Martha Jane rode ahead of the wagons, hunted for buffalo and elk, and became an expert shot. She helped lower the covered wagons over rock ledges in rugged mountains, and forded streams swollen by heavy rains. Martha Jane boasted, "I crossed at the most dangerous spots—just for a thrill!"

Those who knew Martha Jane weren't surprised by her wild ways.

Martha Jane just ignored those who disapproved. Since the day she was born, Martha Jane lived life as she pleased. Actually, it's hard to say exactly when she was born. About 1848 is the best guess, although she claimed her birthday was later and later as she got older and older.

In Virginia City, the Cannary family joined a hillside jumble of tents and shacks 90 miles south of today's Yellowstone Park. The family settled among a throng that harkened from every state east of the Mississippi— and Ireland, Europe, Africa, and Asia. The Virginia City miners washed $30 million worth of gold out of Alder Gulch every year. Although this sounds like a lot, few miners saved a dime, largely because of steep prices. Flour, for example, cost $150 a pound!

It wasn't a pleasant place to live, either. Processing machines clanked and whistled and hummed all day and night. Scraggly sagebrush and

WHICH VIRGINIA CITY?

Just so you are not confused: There were two gold-mining towns called Virginia City (and neither was in the state of Virginia!). The one where Martha Jane lived was in Montana. Another Virginia City, in Nevada, was home to the famous Comstock Load. Legend has it that James Finne (a Virginian) named Virginia City, Nevada, and christened it with a bottle of whisky poured onto the ground. Another early miner named Comstock got the Nevada stream of gold named after him (Comstock Load) because he helped Nevada become a state in 1864. Both the Nevada and Montana towns were rough and rugged places. Mining activity polluted the water. Hurricanes whipped the roofs off houses, and blizzards stranded travelers. Crowded living conditions led to deaths from dysentery, typhus, and malaria. Frostbite and exposure maimed and killed people each winter.

pines provided pitiful protection from fierce winds. Yet big dreamers with high hopes put up with the discomforts.

Because of the inflated prices, it was the merchants, bankers, saloon keepers, cooks, and prostitutes who made most of the real fortunes in Virginia City. Resentment against them often exploded into violence; beatings, shootings, and lynchings were common. Part of the violence was political, too. Most of the merchants—and de facto town leaders— were rabid Union supporters. The Vigilantes, as they called themselves, kept gold flowing to the Union Army and enforced many unwritten laws. Since most of the townsfolk sided with the Confederacy (when President Lincoln was assassinated, deafening cheers rocked Virginia City saloons),

PLACER MINING

Martha Jane's father wasn't digging gold from a mine shaft that tunneled deep in the earth. He was placer mining. A trough called a sluice box, with slats of wood on the bottom, captured water from the river. As the water washed down, gold and gravel dropped through the slats into boxes. The miners picked larger gold nuggets from the gravel, and swirled the rest of the gravel in a pan with tiny holes to catch smaller flakes of gold. Miners got so obsessed with the hunt that they worked in freezing temperatures and lost fingers and toes to frostbite.

PLACER MINING FOR GOLD.

the conflict worsened. Martha Jane witnessed many public shootings and hangings in the violent town.

Only a couple of years after the Cannary family arrived in Virginia City, Martha Jane's parents became sick and died. (No records exist of the cause of their deaths, but diseases such as dysentery and typhus ran rampant in the crowded living conditions.) Local families took in Martha Jane's younger siblings, but she was too old and independent to be looked after. She buried her parents and began her adult adventures, including hanging out with a wild crowd and doing whatever she could to upset the respectable folks in town.

During the 1870s and 1880s, the wild crowd had lots to occupy them in Virginia City and other tattered towns. Twenty-four hours a day, 30,000 residents grubbed for gold, then partied. Then they grubbed and partied some more. The main street sported theaters, saloons, hotels, newspapers, fire companies, a red-light district, and the first miner's union in the United States. Martha Jane had a good time there, but restlessness sent her to Wyoming, Arizona, Nevada, and Dakota, where she worked as a wagoneer and bartender.

On her adventures, Martha Jane began to wear men's clothing, complete with a butcher knife and pistols tucked into her waist belt. It wasn't that Martha Jane was trying to pass herself off as a man—it was more about shock value. Martha Jane got a kick out of needling folks who peered down their noses at her. While she was working in Deadwood, South Dakota, some respectable women grew so offended by Martha Jane's wild ways that they came after her with horsewhips! Martha Jane got away, but not before starting a barroom brawl. Of course, we mainly have Martha Jane's word that such adventures happened. Much in the autobiography she wrote was hugely exaggerated. She claimed to have been a scout for the U.S. Army and a Pony Express driver, for example, but there's no real proof. Probably, she only hauled supplies between Fort Custer, Fort Russell, and Fort Laramie.

It was during those army years that Martha Jane claimed to have been given the nickname of Calamity Jane. Although anything is possible, this likely is a tall tale, too. It goes like this: In 1873, on Goose Creek in South Dakota, Martha Jane was chasing hostile Sioux warriors with some cavalrymen. During an ambush, Martha Jane rescued her wounded captain by cantering into battle and lifting him onto the saddle in front of her. The pair escaped unhurt, although every other soldier died. When the captain recovered, he said, "I name you Calamity Jane, the heroine of the plains."

This story might have a grain of truth to it, but don't forget this: The word *calamity* really means misfortune or affliction. And as Martha Jane grew older, her star faded. So it's far more likely that the name Calamity Jane summed up her downhill slide.

Calamity Jane also told stories about a passionate love affair with Wild Bill Hickock, the famous frontier scout, gambler, and showman. Martha Jane knew the famous Wild Bill (or Buffalo Bill) and performed with him in the *Wild West Show* late in the nineteenth century. Yet there's no proof that she married him and had his child, as she claimed. In fact,

FEMALE OUTLAWS OF THE WEST

Have you read about legendary female outlaws such as Belle Star and Pearl Hart? Most of what you've heard was fabricated by the same novelists and writers who made Calamity Jane famous. About all we really know about Belle Star is that she fell in with a crowd of cutthroat thieves and murderers. Most of the nasty characters with whom she lived, or married, died violently. Her only crime, however, was trading in stolen horses and cattle. In 1889, someone, maybe an angry neighbor, shot her in the back. As for Pearl Hart, she was a Canadian who came to Arizona to rob a single stagecoach in 1899. Pearl saw *Buffalo Bill's Wild West Show* and got more than a little carried away. After a successful robbery and botched getaway, she was arrested and hammed it up for photographers at the jail. They labeled her the "Bandit Queen." After serving her jail time, Pearl disappeared, except for one arrest years later—for stealing canned goods from a grocery store.

Hickock hotly denied it ever happened. Martha Jane married a wagoneer named Clinton Burke in 1885, though, and had a child with him. The daughter born of that match was raised by Saint Mary's Convent in South Dakota, then she disappeared from the public eye.

Hickock's denial of their marriage didn't trouble Martha Jane. She even claimed to have avenged Hickock's death after he was murdered in a Deadwood saloon. Martha Jane said she learned about the killing, tracked the assassin to a butcher shop, and captured him with a meat cleaver!

Along with a terrific imagination, Martha Jane truly had a warm heart. Many people who derided her changed their tune after she nursed the sick and saved lives during a smallpox epidemic. A newspaper even called her an angel of mercy, although they also reported her stints in jail for drunkenness. "To say that the old girl has reformed is something of a chestnut," wrote the Laramie newspaper in 1887. "She was gloriously drunk this morning and if she didn't make Rome howl she did Laramie. Her resting place is now the soft side of an iron cell. Judge Pease will deliver the lecture and collect the fine in the morning."

Addiction to alcohol put a damper on Calamity's later years. The drinking and fighting got so out of hand that she was fired from the *Wild West Show*. When friends tried to help, Martha Jane pushed them away. "Leave me alone and let me go to hell on my own route," she barked.

Calamity Jane's route led to an early death in 1903, but she did not die alone. Good friends stood by her and honored her wish that she be buried next to Wild Bill Hickock in Deadwood. Among those who came to Calamity's funeral was a smallpox victim whom Martha Jane had nursed back to health. The grateful fellow asked to close her coffin before it was lowered into the earth. "She had a rough exterior," the man said, "but a heart of true gold."

CALAMITY JANE LIKE TO SHOCK PEOPLE WITH HER MEN'S CLOTHING AND ROWDY WAYS.

"Stagecoach" Mary Fields

(1 8 3 2 – 1 9 1 4)

Mary Fields of Cascade, Montana, was big, bold—and beloved. A loaded revolver bulged beneath her white apron. A homemade cigar jutted from her mouth. She looked like no man's fool—and she wasn't. In fact, she was one of the toughest characters— male or female—on the American frontier.

Born a Tennessee slave in 1832, Mary headed to the Southwest after the Civil War when she was freed. In Mississippi, she worked as a chambermaid on the steamboat *Robert E. Lee,* which raced the *Natchez* from New Orleans to St. Louis on the Mississippi River. Mary, with the crew, shoved food and furniture into the boiler room to make the fire hotter so that the ship would zip along faster. "It was so blazing hot in the cabins that the passengers took to the decks, and the boilers almost burst," she later told a newspaper reporter. In the end, the *Robert E. Lee* won the race by three and a half hours. Mary was proud when the ship pulled into St. Louis and crowds of people cheered and waved American flags.

AFRICAN AMERICANS IN THE WEST

Did you know that roughly a quarter of cowboys on the frontier were African American? That several all-black towns prospered? That quite a few African Americans became millionaires after striking gold and silver in the mines? It's all true. In the early nineteenth century especially, differences between people mattered less on the frontier than they did back in civilization.

Mary didn't stick with the steamboat long, however. Instead, she took a job offered to her by the mother superior of a convent in Cascade, Montana. At St. Peter's, Mother Amadeus paid Mary $9 a month to oversee the hired hands, help build a school for Native American children, and wash bushel after bushel of nuns' habits. Mary also grew a huge garden that fed the convent and tended several hundred chickens. She was a tough taskmaster, too. When a pesky skunk killed 60 chicks, Mary sneaked up behind with a shovel (to avoid getting sprayed) and did in the enemy. Then she proudly plunked the skunk down on the floor in front of the startled sisters.

Mary drove the convent supply wagons and stagecoach, and local folks began to call her "Stagecoach Mary." With a woolen cap pulled low and a faded apron around her wide waist, Mary became a fixture in Cascade. It was no easy feat hauling guests and supplies through fierce Montana blizzards and

THE NUNS COULDN'T CONVINCE MARY TO GIVE UP HER RIFLE OR ATTEND CHURCH.

downpours to St. Peter's. Packs of hungry wolves could make the runs especially lively. Once a pack spooked the horses, and Mary lost control of the team. After the wagon overturned, Mary guarded the spilled flour and molasses, her rifle cocked and ready. In the morning, the nuns found her wide awake and vigilant.

While Mary hauled supplies, hammered nails, grew vegetables, washed the laundry, and raised her chickens, the sisters ran their Catholic school for Native American children. The nuns tried to convert Mary, too, but she wouldn't even attend mass. Nor could the nuns get her to mend her "wicked" ways, including drinking, swearing, fighting, smoking, and target shooting. Mary, a crack shot, kept shattering bottles lined up on the convent fence posts.

There really was no taming Mary, the nuns learned—not even behind her back. Once when she was away, the nuns crept into her room and gathered some of the ratty old clothes she insisted on wearing. They threw her clothes on a fire, but didn't check the pockets first. In one pocket was a live shotgun cartridge that exploded in the fire. One nun was wounded above her eye. Perhaps they considered it a sign from above, for the nuns didn't try to interfere with Mary's wardrobe again!

Throughout the 1870s, the nuns depended on Mary and nagged her to mend her ways. Once, in an argument over a horse harness, she hit a man in the head with a rock. Another time, she decked a man who called her a nasty name. She even got into a shoot-out with a hired hand at the convent who complained loudly that he wouldn't take orders from a black woman. Luckily, more damage was done to the laundry than anything else. Mary nicked the man's backside, completely ruining his new trousers. The shoot-out also riddled white shirts hanging on the line with bullet holes. Because they were the bishop's shirts—sent from Helena to be laundered—Mary got booted from the convent.

Mary had a loyal friend in Mother Amadeus, however. Not about to cast out Mary haphazardly, Mother Amadeus talked the U.S. Postal Service into giving Mary the Cascade mail route. This suited Mary just fine. With a big cigar in her mouth, she delivered the U.S. mail through rain, snow, sleet, and hail. In the harsh Montana winters, when heavy snowdrifts blocked the narrow roads, Mary tethered the horses and walked.

After several years of driving her route, Mary took a nasty fall. The sisters nursed her back to health—and, at last, convinced her to attend mass. The sisters were so thrilled that they stayed up very late sewing Mary an honorary nun's habit and veil!

CLARA BROWN

Bachelors with grubby jobs depended on laundresses such as Mary Fields and Clara Brown. Clara, of Central City, Colorado, made a fortune by doing laundry and buying into a productive mine. Born in slavery in the South around 1800, Clara was taken from her family at a young age. Later, her own children were sold at auction, too. At age 59, she bought her freedom and traveled by wagon train to Central City, Colorado. For 20 years, Clara never stopped trying to find her lost family. With the money she raised, Clara searched for and found many of the family members she'd been separated from while a slave in the South, including one of her daughters, Eliza. In 1885, Clara made history by becoming the first black member of the Society of Colorado Pioneers.

CLARA BROWN LOST HER FAMILY TO SLAVERY AND USED HER SELF-MADE FORTUNE TO FIND THEM AGAIN.

Mary was still healthy and hearty at age 70, when Mother Amadeus left Montana to establish a mission in Alaska. Mary stayed in Cascade. Too old to carry the mail anymore, she took in laundry.

In her later years, Mary spent a lot of time sitting on downtown park benches, swapping tales with other old-timers. The townspeople honored Mary on her birthday by closing the local school, and when her house burned down, they built her a new one. The town children especially loved Mary, for she knew them all by name, bought them special treats, and cheered them on at ball games. In fact, Mary was a serious baseball fan. Before every game played by the Cascade team, she presented each player with a buttonhole bouquet of flowers from her garden.

When Mary Fields died in 1914, Cascade had grown from a wide and dusty spot in the road to a town with tailoring shops, lawyers' offices, stockyards, banks, hotels, and a dozen saloons. The townsfolk argued over who got to carry the coffin and flocked to her funeral. More than just mourning Mary's death, the people of Cascade were celebrating a rich heritage of diversity by honoring this feisty black woman who lived life courageously and on her own terms.

Sarah Winnemucca Hopkins

(1 8 4 4 – 1 8 9 1)

(Nevada Historical Society)

SARAH WORE HER FINEST PAIUTE DRESS WHEN SHE PLEADED WITH U.S. POLICY-MAKERS TO TREAT THE PAIUTE FAIRLY.

In the early 1880s, Sarah Winnemucca stood before the U.S. Congress dressed in a soft doeskin dress and spoke in a clear, firm voice: "For shame! For shame! You dare to cry out Liberty, when you hold us in places against our will—driving us from place to place as if we were beasts." Sarah pled the cause of her people, the peaceful Paiutes. They had welcomed with open arms the first white people they encountered, then were nearly exterminated by the gold-rush mania. "You have starved my people, broken every promise, told falsehoods," Sarah told the white leaders. "How truly our women prophesied when they told my grandfather that his white brothers would bring sorrow to his people."

Sarah was born in 1844, amid the pine forests along

the Humbolt River in present-day Nevada, near Las Vegas. It was because of her grandfather's friendship with whites that she received the name Sarah. Yet she also was called Paiute names: Thocmetony, which means "shell flower," and Nonooktow, which means "odd child." When she was born her parents believed something quite unusual would be in store for Sarah—and it was. As she grew older, Sarah began to show signs of unique strength. She was fearless and outspoken.

The nomadic Paiutes roamed over a large territory, from southeastern Oregon into Nevada, Idaho, and western Utah. Much of the year, they camped by the wide Humbolt River. On sandbars and pyramid-like rock islands, Sarah played with her friends, some of whom were the children of white settlers.

Since the time her grandfather, Chief Truckee, was a young boy, Sarah's family had maintained a long friendship with white explorers and settlers. Truckee often told his people how, as a youth, he had jumped for joy when he first met the 25 weary explorers led by John C. Fremont and his scout, Kit Carson. The explorers were bone-tired and half-starved after a nine-month journey all the way from Oregon. Luckily for the white men, Paiute legends foretold that the tribe would be reunited with its "lost white relatives." So with open arms, Truckee ushered the explorers into the village and fed them freshly caught trout that made their hungry mouths water.

After Fremont's group was fed and rested, Truckee guided them to California on the trail later named for him. A couple of years later, he returned home, kissed his new granddaughter, Sarah, and told his people about the wonders he'd seen. "There is so much to learn among the white people," he said. In fact, Truckee was so impressed that he moved his family to California for a few years.

In California, Truckee and Sarah's father, Chief Winnemucca,

A PAIUTE STORY

Chief Truckee told his grandchildren a Paiute story that explained why the tribe was so welcoming to the first whites who traveled through their lands. In the beginning of the world, the first man and woman had two girls and two boys, the story went. One girl and boy were dark, and the others were pale. For a time, they got along together without quarreling, but then they argued and fought. The parents saw they must be separated or no one would be happy. They sent the pale children across the ocean, saying that in the future they would return and the rift would be healed. Time passed. The pale children established a great nation across the ocean, and the dark children became the Paiute nation. Then the pale people came home and were reunited with their lost Paiute relatives.

worked on ranches near Santa Cruz and sent Sarah to live with a friendly white family and attend school. She studied first at Saint Mary's Convent School, but whites threatened to remove their daughters if Sarah remained. Then she attended a more welcoming Catholic school in San Jose, where she quickly learned to read and write English. When the family returned home to Nevada a few years later, they sat around the council fire and talked about the white God, better methods of farming, and the Paiutes being part of a great nation called America. Sarah even taught the entire tribe to sing the "Star Spangled Banner."

During the late 1840s and 1850s, however, the friendship with white Americans proved hard to maintain. At first, the Paiutes offered badly needed supplies and shelter to white immigrants who trekked through their land on the Overland Trail. Yet some whites said, "The only good

Indian is a dead Indian," and fired at any Paiute they saw. In one such instance, six Paiute men died, including Sarah's uncle. The tribal council talked of seeking revenge, but the government promised the white men would be punished, so Truckee stood firm for peace.

However, the government did not punish the killers. Then gold was discovered on the tribe's land, and fortune seekers descended by the thousands. The peace was broken, and in the bloody skirmishes that followed the outnumbered Paiutes suffered terrible losses. Many were reduced to begging in the mining camps on their own ancestral land.

Sarah, one of only two Paiutes who could speak English, emerged as a leader of her people. She wrote to the Federal Indian Bureau and asked, "Why do you allow our people's land to be taken? Without land to hunt and gather on, we are starving." Sarah went back and forth as an interpreter and negotiator, translating Paiute complaints to the whites and white promises to the Paiutes.

The government promised food and seed for crops if the Paiutes stayed on the reservation land set aside for them. The Paiutes moved to the reservation, but the promised provisions never arrived, or were of terrible quality. Sarah, trapped between two worlds, was blamed. "You should never have listened to the whites," her people said. "You should tell your people not to be so demanding," the government said.

The Paiutes didn't just want food from the government—they needed it desperately. Whites had chopped down the evergreens the Paiutes counted on for a winter supply of pine nuts, and ranchers shot Paiutes who hunted on "their" land. Fed up at last, the Paiutes went on the warpath and nearly wiped out a white army by Pyramid Lake. Larger white armies took wicked revenge, though, and the Paiutes were herded onto the Malheur reservation, near modern-day Reno. Once again, government agents made soothing noises about peace and promised

DAHTESTE

Many Native American women whose stories have survived were English speakers who worked for peace. It was the only way, many of these women thought, to avoid total extermination of their people. A handful of women were also warriors. Dahteste, the wife of the famous Apache chief Geronimo, started out a respected warrior woman. Yet in the end she also chose negotiation over confrontation. To prevent a bloodbath, Dahteste put down her rifle and negotiated Geronimo's surrender to the U.S. Army (it took 5,000 troops to subdue his small band). The U.S. government did not reward Dahteste, however. Instead, the government sent her to jail for 19 years in Florida, then at Fort Sill, Oklahoma. Amazingly, she survived her imprisonment and lived to a ripe old age on the Mescalero Apache reservation in Arizona.

shipments of food and grain. But neighborhood whites wanted revenge for lost family members and launched sneak attacks. In one, Sarah's mother, sister, and brother were killed.

The terrible bloodshed strained white–Paiute relationships horribly, yet before his death in 1860, Truckee had told his granddaughter to continue standing firm for peace. Despite the death of her family members, Sarah saw little alternative but to do just that. She continued working as a translator and tried to convince her people to give up their nomadic lifestyle, settle for reservation land, and become full-time farmers. She also wrote to government officials in Washington, D.C., and told them that corrupt government agents continued to steal much of the food, farming supplies, and money sent to the reservation.

President Hayes and members of Congress regularly heard from

Sarah. "Friends," she wrote, "we shall never be civilized in the way you wish us to be if you keep on sending us such agents. They do nothing but fill their pockets. Our agent gives my people a third of the grain sent and a third of the hay. My people get no seed for planting or a farmer to help them to plant. The agent threatens to take their wagons away. Year after year, I have told you of the agents' wrongdoing, yet it goes on."

Sometimes, Sarah had an impact. Her pleas spurred Congress to replace crooked agents and pass a special law saying the Paiutes would be repaid for the goods stolen. But distant Washington bureaucrats weren't able to control their agents or enforce their laws out on the frontier. By 1878, broken promises had given birth to a new Paiute leader, Oytes. With his followers (and 150 Bannock warriors who had also left their Idaho reservation), Oytes went on the warpath. When the bloodshed ended (as it always had, in Paiute defeat), all the Paiute and Bannock people were blamed. A small minority had taken up arms, but the army marched all the people at gunpoint, in the dead of winter, to

Fort Simcoe near Yakima, Washington. Several died of exposure along the way.

In Yakima, Sarah and her people suffered frostbite and starvation worse than they'd ever known. Drastic measures were called for, so Sarah traveled to Washington, D.C., to plead for her people. Dressed in Paiute finery, she met with the Secretary of the Interior. "My people have been murdered," Sarah told him. "Our reservations taken from us. Yet we are called blood-seeking savages. How long will you stand by and see us suffer at your hands?" The Secretary of the Interior was moved by Sarah's plea and promised her the Paiutes would be allowed to return to the Malheur reservation. It was yet another promise broken. Instead, the Malheur reservation land was sold to white settlers.

Sarah, however, would not give up! She traveled throughout Nevada and California giving lectures to packed theaters, seeking help for the Paiutes. In a San Francisco audience, an employee of the Indian Department, Lewis H. Hopkins, was deeply moved by Sarah's speech. After the lecture, he introduced himself and a romance blossomed. Within a year, the two were married, and together they traveled to the East again, where Sarah gave more than 300 lectures.

In Boston, Sarah and Lewis found some ardent supporters. Ralph Waldo Emerson, John Greenleaf Whittier, and U.S. Supreme Court Justice Oliver Wendell Holmes all championed her cause. Two influential, intellectual women also threw themselves into lending Sarah a hand. Mary Peabody, married to a famous educator named Horace Mann, was one. The other was Mary's sister, Elizabeth Peabody. The sisters promoted Sarah's lectures, introduced her to influential policymakers, and helped her compile her writings into a book: *Life Among the Paiutes: Their Wrongs and Claims*. Published in 1883, it was the first book written by a Native American woman author. Sarah told of her lifelong struggle to win justice for her people. Many critics of Sarah's book spoke against her, but Sarah just said, "A woman who speaks against bad men will always suffer such criticism."

Unfortunately, support from eastern intellectuals and a popular book did not ease Sarah's personal poverty. Lewis Hopkins was her number-one supporter, but also a heavy burden. In addition to being a gambling addict, he had tuberculosis. Paying his gambling debts and his medical bills ate up all the money Sarah earned from her book.

In the end, however, Sarah's lectures and book did help her people. She stirred up sympathy for the Paiutes, which proved critical. When the Paiutes began escaping from the Yakima reservation and returning to live in their homeland, the government did not interfere. Then, in 1889, legislation restored some of the Paiutes' ancestral land.

After Sarah's husband died of his illness, Sarah returned to live among her people in Nevada. She opened a school for children, which taught them to be proud of Native American traditions and speak the Paiute language. The school was far different from the Indian boarding schools started a few years later by the U.S. government, which taught Native American children to reject their heritage.

In her later years, Sarah retired to live with her sister. Her legacy inspired generations of Paiutes to stand up for their rights, and lawsuits have restored some of the land the tribe lost in the 1800s. The city of Winnemucca, Nevada, proudly bears Sarah's name.

Libbie Custer

(1 8 4 2 – 1 9 3 3)

Galloping across the open plains to hunt buffalo invigorated Elizabeth Custer, the petite, vivacious wife of the famous general George Custer. Libbie, as she was called, was the first army wife to live full-time on frontier army posts. "They call us camp followers, but we are far more than that," she boasted. "Our husbands need us, and we will not be left behind!"

LIBBIE LOVED ART, LITERATURE, FANCY CLOTHES, AND A BOY NAMED GEORGE.

Libbie was her husband's soul mate, social secretary, and press agent all rolled into one. From her own memoirs we can see that she also was a brilliant writer and an adventurer in her own right. She dove headlong into army life and lived to tell the tale. "The wild jolly free life on the frontier suited me," she enthused.

Elizabeth "Libbie" Bacon was born in 1842, the pampered only daughter of a judge in Monroe, Michigan. Daniel Bacon doted on his only child and made sure she got a first-rate education at an elite girls' school. Libbie had a grand wardrobe of the latest fashions from Europe, which absorbed her. But she also loved the study of art and literature.

She could draw like a pro and dance like an angel. No one was surprised when she was named class valedictorian at graduation.

As a young girl, Libbie introduced herself to a wiry blond neighbor boy as he walked by her beautiful home. Perched on the white picket fence, she boldly sassed the jaunty teenager: "Hello, you . . . Custer boy!" Then Libbie left him standing with his mouth hanging open and dashed back into her house.

In 1861, Libbie and George Custer met again at a dance while he was home on leave from West Point. Libbie was smitten by the brash young heartthrob, but threatened never to see him after he staggered past her house drunk. Only after Custer swore that he'd never drink or smoke again did the teetotaling Libbie allow him to court her. According to Libbie, he kept that oath until the day he died.

The romance between George and Libbie heated up quickly. While fighting in Civil War battles, George sent 60-page love letters to Libbie. Yet it wasn't until Custer earned national fame as a Civil War hero—and a promotion at age 23 from captain to brigadier general—that Libbie's protective father would bless the match.

On February 9, 1864, Libbie Bacon and George Custer were married in the Monroe Presbyterian Church. The newlyweds went on a honeymoon romp to Washington, D.C., but it was cut short when George was called to the front. The Union Army of the Potomac was preparing to fight against the Confederate Army of Virginia.

George made plans to send Libbie back home to Monroe, but Libbie told her husband, "I'd rather live in a tent outdoors with you than in a palace with another." George couldn't resist Libbie, so he took her with him to Virginia, where she stayed in a farmhouse near the battle lines. As the cannons roared, Libbie covered her ears and wrote: "I'd insisted on coming along, so I didn't dare express how afraid I was." (In truth, Libbie probably wasn't very afraid. She just liked to act the part of a helpless female.)

George distinguished himself in battle and led soldiers at Gettysburg, Yellow Tavern, Winchester, Five Forks, and in the Appomattox Campaign. Meanwhile, in her temporary quarters near the battle lines, Libbie invited congressmen, senators, and generals to dinner, and she befriended them in her flirtatious yet ladylike way. The big brass loved it—and her—which helped George win friends in high places.

After George's victories for the North helped win the Civil War, General Philip Sheridan presented Libbie with a special gift. It was a table— but not an ordinary one. General Robert E. Lee had sat at the table at Appomattox Court House to write the terms of surrender to the Union. Another memento Libbie took from the war was a wig made for her from the curly blond locks sheared off her husband's head.

Lee's surrender table went with the Custers in 1866, when George returned to the regular U.S. Army and was given the rank of lieutenant colonel. His orders were to march the 4,500-man Southwest Cavalry to duty in Texas and Kansas, which the Custers would call home from 1866 to 1871. The troops were to enforce the Union's efforts to rebuild (and pacify) the defeated South. They also protected white settlers and workers building the new railroads from attacks by hostile Native Americans such as the Cheyenne and Lakota.

In Texas and Kansas, Libbie was basically content. Although bothered by trigger-happy Southern sympathizers who threatened the cavalry, and plantation owners who still traded in slaves despite the Union victory and Emancipation Proclamation, she attended plantation balls hosted by Southern aristocrats. Donning the wig made from her husband's golden locks and dancing until dawn was a welcome change from prairie blizzards, fires, and earthquakes. In the South, Libbie also fell in love with thoroughbred hunting dogs and acquired a half-dozen dogs and puppies that traveled everywhere with the Custers.

Libbie and George were inseparable, especially after one rare stint apart proved disastrous. Libbie had stayed behind at the fort while George campaigned a few hundred miles away. He grew so crabby at being separated from his "pet" that he was cruel to his own men. Then he rode 275 miles to see her without first getting military permission.

Technically, this was desertion—a serious breech of military law—and George was court-martialed. Yet the punishment didn't last long, thanks to friends in high places. George was reinstated and resumed his command with Libbie by his side.

Despite primitive surroundings, Libbie entertained with gusto. She

GEORGE, LIBBIE, AND A SERVANT POSED FOR A FORMAL PORTRAIT.

lined her tents and huts with Mexican shawls called serapes, and invited the officers to share feasts, play cards, hold shooting matches, and go buffalo hunting. "This jolly free life is perfectly fascinating," Libbie wrote to a friend. "We dress as we like and live as we want." As the years passed, more officers' wives joined their husbands in camp after seeing that Libbie was managing just fine.

Although Libbie commanded the social scene, she learned early that military matters were off-limits. The first time she tried get involved, her general husband put her firmly in her wifely place. Libbie had urged a lieutenant who had been robbed by a private to leave camp and hunt the man down. Later, when General Custer learned the lieutenant had left without permission, he was not happy. "I command the regiment, Libbie, not you," he scolded.

In 1871, George was reassigned to Kentucky, to help shut down illegal whisky stills and keep racist posses from spreading their messages of hatred. Libbie, who was a bit of a snob, thought such duties were "unsoldierly." She pined for life in the saddle on the open plain, and so did George. When orders assigned him to Fort Lincoln in Dakota Territory, George whirled Libbie around their tent so ferociously that dishes fell from shelves and shattered. "We had so few household effects that it was a loss," Libbie wrote. "But that didn't seem important just then."

The 1873 move to Dakota was spurred by the discovery of gold in the Black Hills. From the evergreen-darkened hills, Lakota, Sioux, Arickasee, and other tribes had brought gold to trading posts. When the word spread, whites poured onto Native American lands and conflicts erupted. Cavalry units were sent to subdue the hostile tribes.

INDIAN PRINCESS

Libbie and George also paid visits to friendly Native American villages in government-created reservations. Everything about these visits fascinated Libbie, especially the daughter of a chief who dressed like a princess.

"Her feet were moccasined, and her legs and ankles wound round with beaded leggings," the fashion-conscious Libbie wrote. "A blanket drawn over her head was belted at her waist, and she held with great dignity an open parasol. Rows of beads hung about her neck, and broad armlets and anklets of brass adorned her wrists and ankles. Her soft buckskin dress and leggings were heavily embroidered. Her ears were pierced twice—on the side as well as in the lobe—and from these holes were suspended circles of gilt. Her bright eyes, the satin smoothness of her hair, and the clear brown of the skin made a pretty picture."

Dakota felt like Lapland to Libbie because it was so far away, but she threw herself into the move. She plunged kitchen utensils into barrels, bedding into waterproof cloth, and pictures and books into chests. She lovingly packed the childless couple's substitute children—puppies, dogs, caged mockingbirds and canaries—into wagons. Then she joined her husband at the head of a caravan of 900 mounted soldiers. After a steamboat ride to Cairo, Illinois, the regiment took a train as far west as they could go. In wood-paneled Pullman cars lined with large mirrors, plush carpets, and overstuffed chairs, the Custers traveled in style. On stops to water the horses, they frolicked with their dogs.

A REMARKABLE LAUNDRESS

As the grand lady of camp, Libbie sometimes graced the "lower ranks" with her presence. The laundresses who lived in tents along "Suds Row" were among them. On one visit, Libbie met a "tall, course, tender-hearted Mexican woman called Old Nash."

Old Nash, Libbie learned, made a small fortune by moonlighting after she'd finished her washing for the soldiers. She sold pies, sewed, and delivered the babies of soldiers' wives. Nash's husband told Libbie he had chosen a good mate. "She can cook and keeps a right nice home," he said.

Libbie agreed about the cozy home part, for the wife had draped the walls with pink fabric. Carpet also warmed the dirt floor, and polished pots and pans hung from a cupboard she'd built out of wooden crates.

Sometime after her visit, Libbie heard that Old Nash had grown ill and died—and an amazing discovery was made: Old Nash was really a man! How was this kept secret? No one really knows, but it sure was the talk of the frontier fort for a while.

In early April 1873, the cavalry reached the end of the Dakota Southern Railroad and set up a temporary camp in Yankton, Missouri. Other officer's wives—several stayed with their husbands for part of the year—found rooms in a local hotel. Libbie chose to remain in camp, as she usually did.

During the Yankton encampment, Libbie had quite a scare. A nasty prairie blizzard hit suddenly, and Custer ordered his officers to rush Libbie and her servant, Mary, into a half-finished cabin a short distance from the main encampment. The men then left to corral the livestock, but the animal pens collapsed to the ground and were swiftly buried in snowdrifts. General Custer, taken suddenly ill, ordered the soldiers to lead their horses to Yankton; then he collapsed in another cabin.

Meanwhile, Libbie and Mary had no food, water—or roof. They stretched blankets over the rafters, waited, and worried. A half-dozen soldiers who had gotten lost in the storm soon joined them. As the snow drifted to the tops of the windows, Libbie wrapped the freezing men in more blankets. Outside, lost dogs, hogs, mules, and horses howled, brayed, whinnied, and squealed. "It was simply terrible," Libbie wrote. "We were forgotten castaways, hidden under the drifts that surrounded us."

The good people of Yankton hadn't forgotten about them, though. A rescue party dug them out and hurried them to town. When Libbie was safely tucked away in her hotel room, she cried for the men who suffered amputations due to frostbite (and because her puppies had died in the storm). Her rare tears won Libbie a lecture. "My dear, you must not give way to weakness," her husband scolded. "Pull yourself together and be a good example to others." Libbie took the lecture to heart and dried her tears. "After that, I drilled myself to never be too cold, too hot, too hungry—or inconvenient to anyone," she wrote.

After surviving the blizzard, the caravan moved on to Dakota on horseback. The bugler played "Boots and Saddles," as each mounted soldier took his place in line, two abreast. The general, his staff, and Libbie led the cavalcade. Following them were the companies, supply wagons, and rear guard.

This was Libbie's longest march yet, and she learned a few important lessons. She learned not to drink much water because rest stops were few—and to grab a quick nap when the caravan stopped for lunch. The minute Libbie was helped out of the saddle, she stretched her cramped leg muscles. If no other shade was to be had, Libbie crept under a wagon and shared that spot with the dogs. Once she woke to find her dogs barking at a huge rattlesnake slithering toward her—and realized why Native American women tied their swaddled infants to tree limbs at nap time.

Despite the naps, when evening rolled around Libbie was thoroughly exhausted. After a reviving supper, though, she and George had their happiest times. Soldiers pulled wagons in a circle, pitched tents in two long lines facing each other, tied up the horses, chopped wood, hauled water, and lit fires. A soldier played the accordion as the hounds bayed and the troops sang and traded stories.

At last, the cavalry reached Fort Abraham Lincoln, near present-day Bismarck. Custer and his men guarded surveyors for the Northern Pacific Railroad and tried to pacify the Sioux. Along with barracks for soldiers, a parade ground, houses for officers, stables, and quarters for the laundress and native scouts, there was a fort store. Attached to the store was a billiard room, barbershop, and photographer's studio.

Libbie's own house was made of warped lumber that left big gaps in the wall. A stand held George's pistols, hunting knives, muskets, and sabers. His hunting trophies hung on the walls, including the heads of buffalo, grizzly bears, antelopes, and deer. Deer antlers served as hooks

RIDING DRESS

Women on the trail quickly abandoned troublesome and restricting garments such as corsets and hooped skirts, but few could bring themselves to switch from riding sidesaddle to riding astride. Few traded their skirts for pants, either. Wide Turkish pants—gathered at the bottom and called bloomers after their creator, Amelia Bloomer—just didn't catch on. Instead, some women sewed rocks into their skirt hems to keep them from flying about in high winds, or they wore men's pants under their dresses. By the late 1800s, some women opted for "split pants," which looked like a cross between a dress and pants.

for spurs, riding whips, caps, field glasses, and compasses. The tables and desks were littered with stuffed owls, eagles, and foxes, and the hides of bear, beaver, and mountain lions warmed the floor. Surrounded by his gear and trophies, General Custer found time to write some magazine articles and a book titled *My Life on the Plains*.

In the summer of 1876, Libbie's frontier adventures ended abruptly and tragically. Custer's Seventh Cavalry unit was called out to subdue hostile warriors united under Sitting Bull. As 1,200 men rode into a misty morning, Libbie joined them for a while. When she turned back to the fort, the band struck up "The Girl I Left Behind Me."

Libbie expected George to be back, safe and sound, in a couple of weeks. Yet when she learned that another large detachment had been attacked by Sitting Bull's warriors, she began to fret. In the middle of the night on July 5, Libbie's worry turned to grief. Captain William McCaskey knocked at Libbie's back door and gave her news that her husband and 250 other men had been killed in the Battle of Little

Bighorn. Libbie grew pale as a ghost, but did not cry. Instead, she threw a cloak over her nightgown and went to break the news to the other widows at Fort Lincoln.

After her husband's death, Elizabeth Bacon Custer left the frontier for New York City. Many blamed her husband—unfairly or fairly—for the shameful military defeat at Little Bighorn, so Libbie picked up her pen and set to work portraying George Custer as an American hero.

In magazines and books, Libbie portrayed General George Armstrong Custer as a brilliant military leader, a cultivated man, and a devoted husband. Because Libbie was a dynamite writer who described the frontier in living color, she succeeded in creating a larger-than-life hero admired by generations to come. While Libbie lived, no one dared challenge this view. Her books about her own adventures—*Boots and Saddles* (1885) and *Following the Guidon* (1890)—also were popular. The debt-ridden widow quickly transformed herself into a well-off author.

Even in death, Libbie promoted her beloved George. In her will,

Libbie left General Custer's boots, which had trudged from the Mexican to Canadian borders, to the Museum of History in Topeka, Kansas.

THE BATTLE OF LITTLE BIGHORN

The Battle of Little Bighorn was a dreadful defeat for American forces. The public wanted to know how and why an entire unit of the U.S. Cavalry had been wiped out. The answer is hard to simplify. In fact, in the 125 years since the battle, thousands of books and articles have been written analyzing it! Nevertheless, this summary may be helpful.

The American soldiers had a formidable foe in the united Lakota Sioux, Arapaho Cheyenne, and other Native Americans who united to boot settlers, miners, and the army out of the sacred Black Hills. Their leader was the famous Sioux chief, Sitting Bull. Gold had been discovered in the area (present-day Idaho, South Dakota, and Montana). Miners were descending like flies, and the U.S. government was about to build a road that would disrupt the buffalo hunting. The army sent three columns of soldiers against the warriors, including several hundred men in General Custer's Seventh Cavalry. On the way, Custer attacked a large Sioux encampment even though there were three times as many warriors as cavalrymen. (Scouts may have undercounted, or Custer may have been overconfident.) The lay of the land wasn't ideal for an attack, either. In the end, the 210-man company led by Custer was forced against a ridge with no escape route. The cavalrymen shot their horses and made a wall from the corpses, but in less than an hour every man was killed.

Although the Battle of Little Bighorn was a great victory for the Native American army, treaties that followed restricted the Native Americans to reservations and opened the Black Hills to settlement.

CHAPTER 13

Nellie Cashman

(1 8 ? ? – 1 9 2 5)

(Alaska State Library/Historical Collections/01-4024)

NELLIE OPERATED RESTAURANTS AND HOTELS IN MINING CAMPS FROM ARIZONA TO ALASKA.

N ellie Cashman, a desperately poor immigrant from Ireland, traveled through the frontier opening restaurants and hotels, mining land, chastising the drunken, rescuing the stranded, mothering orphans, and feeding the downtrodden. Along the way, this beloved frontier legend acquired more nicknames than you can count, including Saint of the Sourdoughs, Miner's Angel, Angel of the Cassair, and Angel of Tombstone.

Nellie spent her early childhood in County Cork, Ireland, where she was born. She went to bed hungry. The potato crop her family once depended on had withered in the fields. Without crops, poor farmers who rented land from rich landlords couldn't pay their rents. Many tenant farmers were evicted and roamed the roads begging for morsels of food. Things were even worse for Nellie after her father died, when she was still a toddler.

Poverty wasn't the only problem afflicting Nellie's widowed mother, Frances. Like most tenant farmers, Nellie's family was Catholic, and Protestant Britain ruled Ireland. They didn't allow Irish Catholics to own land, vote, or even attend mass. This combination of religious oppression and poverty fostered fierce rebellions. Uprisings against the landholding lords were common and bloody. Young Nellie Cashman probably saw the British soldiers, as they marched through Queenstown, carrying the heads of executed Irish rebels on spikes. It was a common sight.

Desperate but determined, Frances Cashman fixed on the tales being told all over Ireland of America's wealth. People said that in America the wheat practically planted itself and pigs roamed the streets, ready to be plucked up and cooked for supper! Somehow, Frances scraped together money for the long ocean voyage in 1845. She packed the family's gear and sailed with Nellie and Nellie's younger sister, Fanny, on a cramped immigrant ship bound for Boston.

Thankfully, food was more plentiful in America, but eastern cities teemed with immigrants. Instead of spacious homes on plots of land, the immigrants crammed into stuffy slums. Jobs were scarce and wages were low. Nellie grew up poor in Boston, yet she refused to let that keep her down. In fact, nothing ever stopped her, as the world would soon find out!

While still a young girl, Nellie landed a steady job as a bellhop at a ritzy Boston hotel. She befriended everyone she met there, including General Ulysses S. Grant. "Go West, Nellie!" General Grant told her. "Girls like you are needed there!"

Those words stuck with Nellie, as did tales of fortunes being made in frontier gold and silver mines. By the early to mid-1860s, Nellie had saved enough money to head for the frontier. For the next 60 years, she jumped from mining camp to mining camp in Nevada, Colorado, California, Arizona, and Alaska.

Nellie quickly learned that only a few lucky miners made fortunes; the rest camped out in filthy shacks, scraping together only enough gold nuggets to pay for food and whisky. It was the businesspeople who catered to the miners who raked in the steadiest profits. In Nevada, Nellie first made a mint cooking for hungry miners and then opened a boardinghouse.

Rough living in a lawless land made for some hard-bitten men. Drinking, gambling, and gun fights filled most miners' nights; and some business owners couldn't control the rowdy ne'er-do-wells. But Nellie could! When Nellie said, "No fighting in my place, lads," she was obeyed. If some dunderhead dared to talk back to Nellie, another man jumped up and tossed him into the street. On the outside, Nellie seemed tough, but on the inside she was a devout Catholic with a kind heart. "The Miners' Angel" gave free food, shelter, and loans to scores of orphans, widows, and destitute miners. Many other independent frontier women were accused of being wanton hussies (whether they deserved it or not). But the respect Nellie commanded was legendary.

Sometimes that respect was accompanied by love, for she was a real looker and had plenty of suitors. Black curls framed a pale pixie face with dancing black eyes. Nellie could have had her pick, but she was more fond of bossing wild men around than marrying them. Also, her feet itched to ramble, not to raise babies and settle down.

When Nellie heard that gold was streaming from the earth in Alaska and British Columbia, she sold her hotel and made plans to venture north. It was frigid way up north, and Nellie was much too practical to

ALASKAN GOLD RUSH

Gold mining wasn't all was it cracked up to be. Of 100,000 people who headed to Alaska in the last gold rush, only 30,000 actually made it. Fifteen thousand managed to mine for gold. About 4,000 found a little bit of gold and only a few hundred made fortunes. Others worked for wages, opened businesses, or dejectedly made their way back home. In the end, about $22 million of gold came out of the area.

MINING CAMP ENTREPRENEURS WERE FAR MORE LIKELY TO GET RICH THAN THE MINERS.

travel across snow-packed mountain passes in a dress! So she stocked up on supplies and warm clothes, including a men's fur coat and hat.

Few of the thousands of miners already there had been as practical as Nellie. When she got to the Cassair region of British Columbia (near Alaska), she found thousands of poorly clothed men with empty bellies. Their vest pockets bulged with gold, but they had lost fingers to frostbite and were nearly dead of starvation. Naturally, Nellie got busy selling clothes and food to the eager, desperate bachelors—and taking their gold. (To those men without a dime to their names, of course, she gave supplies away.)

After making a mint selling supplies, Nellie worked at saving souls. She gave much of her money to the Catholic Church for a much-needed hospital. She also worked her own gold-mine claims—and protected them fiercely. Lawsuits over who owned lands and mines clogged the courts, and Nellie filed her share.

Nellie hadn't been in the Northwest long when she earned the nickname "Angel of Cassair." Miners in the Cassair Mountains were snowed in without supplies, and everyone said the drifts were too high to get through. But they were not too high for Nellie! Without hesitation, she bought several dogsleds, packed them with food, medicine, and blankets, and convinced six men to go with her to rescue the miners. It took several days, but the rescuers got through. The *Victoria Daily British*

BELINDA MELROONEY

Nellie Cashman was one of several notable female entrepreneurs in the Pacific Northwest. Among them was Belinda Melrooney, also a native of Ireland. Legend has it that when Belinda arrived in Dawson, Alaska, she threw her last 50 cents into a river and swore she would never again need such small change. Eventually, she would run a dress shop, restaurant, and hotel. At the Fairview Hotel near Dawson, her bar made $6,000 on opening day. Unlike Nellie, Belinda married—but she probably shouldn't have! Her husband, the "French count," turned out to be a liquor salesman in disguise. He stole her furs and jewels, but Belinda was still rich when she retired to live out her years in Yakima, Washington.

Colonist of February 5, 1875, noted that Nellie Cashman was a bit insane—but a hero to be sure.

For five years, Nellie lived in the frigid north, catered to miners, worked her claims, made money, and gave it away. Then boomtowns in Arizona drew her south. During the 1880s, in Tucson and Tombstone, the sought-after mineral was silver. Nellie owned a few claims and operated a restaurant called Russ House. (Her advertisement read: "There are no cockroaches in my kitchen and the flour is clean.")

In Tombstone, Nellie got even the toughest characters to do her bidding. She convinced the lawman, Wyatt Earp, to close his Crystal Palace saloon on Sunday so that church services could be held there. Of course, that was just until she'd raised enough funds to build a church, as well as another hospital. Nellie was always passing the hat to collect funds for worthy causes.

In 1883, news of a gold strike in Baja, California, lured Nellie away again. She lead a group of veteran prospectors south by train into Mexico, sailed across the Gulf of California, then headed for Baja desert. This time, there was no gold—and the desert heat nearly killed everyone! Despite the failed adventure, not one of the men blamed Nellie. From beginning to end, she was the undisputed leader of the pack.

After her return to Arizona, Nellie found herself with five new mouths to feed. Nellie's widowed sister, Fanny, died of tuberculosis. She left behind her children for Nellie to raise, and, of course, Nellie threw herself into the task. Parenthood also may have turned her into a crusader, for she set about trying to reform a custom she'd long thought barbaric—public hangings. When angry miners tried to lynch the superintendent of the Grand Central Mining Company, Nellie spirited him away. She also organized a group to tear down the bleachers built around a scaffold big enough to hang five men.

By 1897, the old frontier had become far too civilized for Nellie. Once again, Alaska called. By this time, her adopted children were grown and settled, but one nephew, Tom Cunningham, traveled with her. Together they opened a restaurant (free cigars lured customers) and a grocery store. They also worked several isolated mines, and even in her old age, Nellie mushed her team of dogsleds hundreds of miles from one claim to another.

In 1923, a reporter came to interview Nellie, who had moved to nearby British Columbia. "Why didn't you ever marry?" the brazen young man asked gray-haired Nellie. "Why, child," Nellie answered, "I haven't had time for marriage. Men are a nuisance anyhow, now aren't they? They're just boys grown up." Two years later, in 1925, Nellie died of pneumonia at St. Joseph's Hospital in British Columbia—a hospital she had helped fund years before.

THE MIDNIGHT SUN MINING COMPANY

For awhile Nellie worked a claim even farther north—only 60 miles from the Arctic Circle. The Koyukuk Wilderness drew the toughest loners alive, including some escaped criminals. Only a half-dozen women lived in the area, and most were prostitutes. None of this fazed Nellie, who was still after the Big Bonanza (if only to give it away). Alongside a couple of hired hands, she organized the "Midnight Sun Mining Company" and offered 50,000 shares for $2 each. Although she didn't hit the bigtime, the venture paid for itself and then some.

Evelyn Cameron

(1 8 6 8 - 1 9 2 8)

By 1889, when 21-year-old Evelyn Cameron stepped off the train in eastern Montana, the American frontier was famous worldwide as an exotic, untamed wilderness. Newlyweds Evelyn and Evan Cameron were honeymooning British tourists who came to see the sights and have an adventure. The aristocratic Camerons had done their travel planning well. At a time when the frontier was rapidly becoming a thing of the past—Native Americans lived on reservations; in many areas, wild animals were nearly extinct; and cultivated fields replaced untouched landscapes—eastern Montana, with its formidable terrain and climate, remained one of the least inhabited, wildest places left in America. Evelyn had come for a vacation, but she fell head-over-heels in love with the land and people. She stayed until her death and became a Montana legend.

Evelyn Flowers was born in 1868 to a wealthy English family and was raised in a sprawling stone house on a large country estate south of

London. She rode sidesaddle in elegant riding outfits complete with gloves and a derby hat. At age 21, Evelyn displeased her high-toned family by marrying a book-loving Scotsman, Evan Cameron. He was 15 years older than she and had health problems that made him physically weak. Her family wasn't pleased by the match, but Evelyn tended to get her way.

Romantic tales, adventure novels, and travel writing drew the Camerons to the American frontier. Some said the Montana badlands and plains, with their cyclones, hailstorms, and droughts, were desolate and harsh. Evelyn, however, found the wide skies, sandstone rock formations, and windblown grasses breathtaking.

The Camerons brought a cook and a guide with them on their honeymoon. They hunted a little game, watched birds with their binoculars,

WOMEN WRITERS ON THE FRONTIER

In the late 1800s, photographers found a wealth of material on the frontier—and so did writers. Women writers contributed to dozens of newspapers and wrote books about everything from crusading investigations to fluffy romances. Helen Hunt Jackson, who came to Colorado Springs for the climate, ended up caring deeply about Native American rights. In 1881, she wrote *A Century of Dishonor: A Sketch of the United States Government's Dealings with Some of the Indian Tribes.* Mary Hallock Foote of Idaho wrote *The Led-Horse Claim* in 1883 about a young man and woman from families with rival mining claims who fall in love. For 30 years, Bertha Muzzy Sinclair of Montana (pen name: B. M. Bower) wrote romance novels set in ranching communities. In *Chip of the Flying U,* an injured cowboy falls in love with a woman doctor from the East.

enjoyed the vivid sunsets, and gazed at the star-filled sky by night. They didn't mind the hot days and chilly nights. With each passing day, Evelyn loved Montana more and wanted to stay. Evan shared her feelings.

Although from well-off families, the Camerons weren't wealthy themselves. To stay in the United States, they needed a livelihood, and Evan came up with a plan to raise polo ponies and export them to England. They rented some land and a cabin, imported some breeding stock, and got to work.

At first, the Camerons rented a cabin on the Powder River, just east of Miles City. Then they bought Eve Ranch, just south of the railroad town of Terry. With its bullet-riddled saloon and dirt streets, Terry was a far cry from anything Evelyn had seen in England. But she didn't seem to mind a bit. To her sister in England, she wrote: "Terry has been rather lively of late, cowboys shooting here, there & and everywhere. One saloon is riddled with bullet holes. In fact, someone painted the town red & no one was arrested!"

Unfortunately, Evan made poor investments, and the pony-raising venture failed. Within a few years, the Camerons were nearly broke. Evan thought their only choice was to go home to England, but Evelyn said that would be too humiliating. She wrote in her diary, "I don't care about home [England] now. I feel as though I would like to never hear nor go near it."

Like many other financially strapped women, Evelyn began taking in borders to help make ends meet. One of them introduced her to photography, and Evelyn loved it. Before long, a new career was born.

In 1894, Evelyn bought a mail-order camera and took up photographing Montana's people, wildlife, and landscape. Camera in tow, she shot images that captured the daily lives of cowboys, hunters, sheep shearers, ranchers, farm wives, dance-hall girls, and golden eagles. She sold her pictures for 25 cents each, or $3 a dozen. She also turned the images into postcards to sell, then sold albums to hold the postcards.

Evelyn did well with her photographs, but there wasn't enough business in Montana for a full-time career. Evelyn had to combine it with ranching (raising cattle, horses, and sheep), selling vegetables, and cooking for ranch hands. Because her husband was not well, the work was her responsibility. She abandoned her aristocratic roots, rolled up her sleeves, and happily ditched her dress for a split skirt. In the wide-legged skirt, she rode like a man, astride the horse instead of in a sidesaddle. Often, she went hatless, too, and let her hair hang in a windblown ponytail. Exposed to the sun and wind, her skin grew leathery brown.

Some hardworking frontier women who found full skirts heavy and awkward switched to wearing split skirts, which were also called divided garments. They looked enough like dresses to hide the shape of women's legs, yet they were more practical. Prejudice against them was fierce, though. When Evelyn went to the nearby town of Miles City, the local

EVELYN'S DIARY, OCTOBER 7, 1899

Arose 5:50. Jan [the dog] woke me out of a deep sleep scratching at our door to be let out. Breakfast started. Fed chicks and milked Roanie. Cut up [Roanie's] squashes and cucumbers. Breakfast at 8:40. . . . Cleaned our room. Skinned out a little horned owl for Evan. Began to wash 12:15. Lunch 1:40. . . . Worked up sponge [yeast] into dough. . . . Made dough into loaves. Printed 5 [negative plates] and spotted plates. . . . 2 [plates] require too much doctoring [for scratches] to print from. This made me late getting washing done. 1 sheet, 7 towels, 8 dish cloths, 3 pillow cases, 2 aprons, 2 blouses, 6 flannel shirts, 2 vests, 1 pair drawers, 2 flannel combis, 4 pair socks, 1 nightgown. . . . Scrubbed floor; baked and put supper on. 4:40 Fed pups. Fed chicks. Milked. . . . I churned after supper 2 lbs., 4 ounces butter. Wrote diary.

girls stared and laughed at her split skirt. A Miles City lawman threatened to arrest her for her scandalous attire!

What might have been a prison of drudgery to another woman brought Evelyn tremendous joy. She was blessed with a positive outlook on life and discovered a deep love for manual labor. "It's all I care about," she wrote. "I like to break colts, brand calves, cut down trees, ride, and work in the garden."

It's amazing that Evelyn found time to shoot photographs given her packed daily schedule, especially because she didn't have a studio for shooting formal portraits. Instead, she traveled the countryside and took pictures of people in their homes, yards, stables, and fields. She documented her subjects' daily lives, as they ate supper, broke horses, and threshed wheat. She also photographed lots of wildlife, including a

golden eagle's nest that held two eggs. Several times, Evelyn climbed a steep cliff to photograph the eagle's nest and its eggs, then the mother and babies after they were born. The eagle family grew so familiar with her that they eventually let her pick them up and pose them in photographs!

An abiding interest in wildlife and their habitats grew out of Evelyn's photography work. With her husband, she catalogued the populations of Swainson's hawks, blue herons, phalaropes, golden eagles, and other birds. The Cameron home also became an animal hospital for the wounded, including grizzly cubs, antelope, hawks, and wolves. (The wolf pups liked to pick up the ranch's kittens and carry them around in their mouths!)

In 1918, Evelyn's husband died of cancer, and she carried on alone. For 13 years, she continued her photography business while running the ranch. When tourists came to the area to see the sights, people said, "Visit

Evelyn. She is one of the wonders of Montana." Yet, outside of eastern Montana, no one ever heard of Evelyn Cameron. Only local folks attended her funeral when she died in 1928 of heart failure.

Fifty years after her death, an editor working on a book about pioneer women discovered Evelyn Cameron's photographic work tucked away in the basement of Evelyn's old Montana ranch house. There were 1,800 dust-covered glass-plate and film negatives and 2,500 original photographs. Today, in museums throughout Montana, you can see Cameron's fantastic visual record of frontier life for yourself.

WOMEN PHOTOGRAPHERS

As early as the 1840s, female professional photographers hung out their shingles in cities such as New York, Boston, and San Francisco. Cameras were large, boxy things then, with bellows that looked like accordions, and heavy glass-plate negatives. Commercial photographers carried the plates on pack mules and developed the prints in wagons. It wasn't until the 1880s that flexible film and smaller cameras were invented.

In 1888, Eastman-Kodak launched a nationwide advertising campaign featuring the "Kodak Girl." After that, more women took up photography as a hobby and profession. Photography was an acceptable career for women because it was trendy and artistic. Also, since it was a new career, it was easier for women to get in on the ground floor. By 1900, roughly a quarter of America's professional photographers were women.

SUGGESTED READING

Alter, Judy. *Women of the Old West.* New York: Franklin Watts, 1989.

Faber, Doris. *Calamity Jane: Her Life and Her Legend.* Boston: Houghton Mifflin, 1992.

Ferris, Jeri Chase. *With Open Hands: A Story About Biddy Mason.* Minneapolis: Lerner Publishing Group, 1998.

Katz, William Loren. *Black Women of the Old West.* New York: Athenaeum Books for Young Readers, 1995.

Ketchum, Liza. *Into a New Country: Eight Remarkable Women of the West.* New York: Little Brown & Co., 2000.

Levine, Ellen. *If You Traveled West in a Covered Wagon.* New York: Scholastic Trade, 1992.

McGowen, Tom. *African-Americans in the Old West.* New York: Children's Press, 1999.

Miller, Marie Brandon. *Buffalo Gals: Women of the Old West.* Minneapolis: Lerner Publishing Group, 1995.

Miller, Robert. *The Story of Stagecoach Mary Fields.* Parsipanny, N.J.: Silver Burdett Press, 1994.

Pelt, Ruth. *Women of the Wild West.* North Carolina: Open Hand Publishing, 1994.

Scordato, Ellen. *Sarah Winnemucca: Northern Paiute Writer and Diplomat.* Broomall, Penn.: Chelsea House, 1992.

Sigerman, Harriet. *Land of Many Hands: Women in the American West.* New York: Oxford University Press Childrens Books, 1997.

St. George, Judith. *Sacagawea.* New York: Philomel Books, 1997.

Wilson, Ellen Cameron. *Annie Oakley: Young Markswoman.* New York: Aladdin Paperbacks, 1989.

Page 5: courtesy of the Denver Public Library, Western History Collection, Call #X-33784; page 9: courtesy of Oregon Historical Society, OHS Neg #ORH527; page 15: courtesy of Perry-Castaneda Map Collection, University of Texas at Austin; page 16: Bettman/Corbis; page 19: courtesy of National Park Service, Whitman Mission National Historical Site; page 26: courtesy of the Denver Public Library, Western History Collection, Call # N-328; page 28: courtesy of Los Altos History Museum; page 41: courtesy of the Denver Public Library, Western History Collection, Call #F26809; page 48: Special Collections and Archives, Merrill Library, Utah State University; pages 52, 75, 88, and 100: courtesy of National Archives; page 55: courtesy of the California History Room, California State Library, Sacramento, California; page 57: courtesy of Seaver Center for Western History Research, Los Angeles County Museum of Natural History; pages 66 and 73: Library of Congress; page 77: Hulton/Archive; page 79: Archives, Ursuline Convent of the Sacred Heart, Toledo, Ohio; page 81: courtesy of the Denver Public Library, Western History Collection, Call #Z275; page 91: courtesy of the Denver Public Library, Western History Collection, Call #B-942 1874; page 94: courtesy of the Little Bighorn Battlefield National Monument/National Park Service; page 105: Corbis; page 112: courtesy of the Montana Historical Society; page 114: courtesy of Prairie County Museum, Terry, Montana.

Mary Elizabeth Achey. For 20 years, Mary Elizabeth Achey traveled with her two young children, painting frontier scenes in Missouri, Colorado, California, Oregon, and Washington. Like Libbie Custer, she'd come to the frontier in the 1860s as an army wife, but when her only daughter died of fever, she blamed her husband and struck out on her own. From 1860 to 1885, when she died at age 53, she traveled the frontier painting army posts, mining camps, and landscapes.

Margaret "Unsinkable Molly" Brown. In the late 1800s, Molly and her husband struck it rich mining for gold in Leadville, Colorado. They moved to San Francisco and built a mansion. Molly tried to fit in with the other rich folks, but she was too flamboyant. Nevertheless, she enjoyed her wealth, and with some of it she took a ride on the *Titanic.* She survived that ship's sinking in 1912, and showed real heroism in the lifeboat. Newspapers dubbed her the "Unsinkable Molly Brown."

Abigail Scott Duniway. At age 17, in 1852, Abigail Scott traveled with her family in a covered wagon from Illinois to Oregon. She married, gave birth to six children, ran a homestead, and then became a successful milliner (hat maker) after her husband was disabled. She also wrote a novel about the overland journey, *From the West to the West.* Eventually, Abigail would write several novels, but it was as a crusader and newspaper publisher that she made her true mark. In the 1870s, she embraced the cause of women's suffrage and published a weekly newspaper, the *New Northwest,* in which she espoused her views. When Susan B. Anthony visited the Pacific Coast, the two gave lectures together.

Clara Foltz. In 1878, Clara Foltz lobbied successfully for an amendment to the California Constitution that allowed women to become lawyers, then was admitted to the California bar as the first woman licensed to practice law. In San

Diego, Denver, and New York, she practiced law. To men who told her a woman's place was in the home, she always said, "A woman would better be almost anyplace than home raising men like you." Foltz also made history as the first female deputy district attorney in Los Angeles and fought for women's voting rights.

Molly Goodnight. Tennessee-born Molly Goodnight was married to a renowned Texas rancher, Charles Goodnight. On a half-million isolated acres—in the 1,500-foot-deep, 10-mile-wide, 100-mile-long Palo Duro Canyon—the childless couple made a small fortune. Sometimes Molly didn't see a neighbor for six months, but the ranch was a little village all its own. The residents were the dozens of rough-and-ready cowboys who managed 60,000 head of cattle on the open range. They weren't always easy to keep in line, but for Molly they'd do anything. Molly had a cause that occupied her, too. She worked passionately to rescue and protect baby buffalo left to die after hunters killed their parents. She created the Goodnight Buffalo Herd, and some she crossbred with range cattle to produce "Cattalo."

Bethenia Owens-Adair. A child among the settlers who followed the Whitman Trail to Oregon, Bethenia Owens was married at age 14, gave birth to a son at 16, then left her abusive husband at 18. After shocking her parents with this unheard-of independence, she stunned them further by doing quite well for herself as a single working woman. She nursed the sick and ran a school. In the 1880s, after her son was raised, she graduated from a Michigan medical school, then returned to practice medicine throughout Oregon and Washington.

Esther Pariseau. The Canadian Esther Pariseau became "Mother Joseph," and in 1856 led five missionaries to the Pacific Northwest. Mother Joseph founded hospitals and several schools and orphanages in present-day Washington, northern Oregon, Idaho, and Montana. She designed the buildings, raised funds from miners, and was a tough taskmaster for the building crews (she bounced on planks to make sure they were strong enough). In 1953, the American Institute of Architects dubbed her the first architect of the Pacific Northwest.

Susan LaFlesche Picotte. The daughter of Chief Joseph of the Omaha tribe left Nebraska to attend college and medical school in the East. The tradition of being educated in white schools stemmed from Susan's mixed cultural ancestry. Her mother was Iowa, Omaha, and English; her father was French and Omaha. In 1889, Susan graduated first in her class and returned to teach and practice medicine on the reservation. She also built a hospital that served both Native Americans and whites. Through lectures and writings, Susan generated national concern for Native American rights.

Natasha Shelikof. In 1784, the first manager of Russian Alaska (Russia sold Alaska to the United States in 1867) was Gregory Shelikof. On a convoy of three sailing ships, Shelikof brought only one woman with 192 men: his wife, Natasha. She managed the colony's farm, taught Native women, and joined fur-hunting parties to islands in Prince William Sound. She also nearly froze to death on such journeys, more than once. When her husband went on long hunting trips alone, Natasha was in charge of the colony.